Who hasn't asked the question: "Why did God create a world with so much turmoil and pain?" The answer Jay Payleitner gives in his new book *Checking the Boxes Only You Can Check: 40 Ways to Make the World a Better Place* is that God created *you* to do something about it. Jay's invigorating book shows how you can be a person who helps overcome the troubles of the world, starting within yourself, checking one box at a time.

—*Edward Grinnan*
Editor-in-chief and vice president, Guideposts

I agree with Jay that *"the world works best when humanity is looking for answers, not pointing fingers or passing the buck."* This book really resonates with me as a man. I desperately want to make a difference for good, and Jay encourages me with solid reminders of how to do just that.

—*Brian Doyle*
Founder and president, Iron Sharpens Iron

With *Checking the Boxes Only You Can Check,* Jay has created an empowering guide, encouraging readers to embrace personal responsibility and kickstart their impact on the world through practical, Scripture-based wisdom. A truly uplifting read for those seeking to embrace the journey toward living an excellent life with purpose and self-awareness.

—*Anne Nelson*
Founder and CEO, Fully Thriving

We all mean well and want to leave the mark of Christ on our family and our broader sphere of influence. Once again, Jay gives us helpful insights and tools to do just that.

—*Grady Hauser*
Author, *Passing the Baton: 100 Life Principles and Skills Every Father Needs to Teach His Children*

I picked up Jay's book, *Checking the Boxes Only You Can Check*, thinking that it might be a helpful book for passing biblical lessons and values on to our children and grandchildren. While that's indeed true, I was immediately impressed that I needed to first check the boxes myself. We can't pass on what we don't have.

—*Wayne Shepherd*
Christian radio host

Jay Payleitner is one of the most creative writers I know. *Checking the Boxes Only You Can Check* is another example of his creative genius. This is not a book about bucket lists that make us feel good about ourselves. It's not about bragging rights either. No, Jay writes so we don't forget that God made us on purpose with a purpose. It's a reminder to embrace God's plans He has already prepared for us as His masterpieces to impact our world through the aroma of Christ.

—*Cavin Harper*
Founder and CEO, ElderQuest Ministries

This is sensible, simple, and easy to digest...a must read if you are looking for a way to improve your relationships and yourself!

—*Jeffrey K. Butcher*
President emeritus, Brotherhood of St. Andrew USA

Do you want your life to go somewhere? To make a difference in your world? Here's your preflight checklist. Or rather your in-flight checklist to a God-centered, difference-making life.

—*Leary Gates*
Venture leadership coach and founder, Strategic CEO

A witty and no-punch-pulled narrative that should convict the most seasoned believer. Our role as Christ followers is to bring the shalom of the kingdom of God to this darkened world. In other words, make it a better place. In true Jay style, he checks the boxes with forty well-defined ways to do just that. Read on, friends. Our time is short, no fence-sitters allowed.

—*Steve Adams*
Executive director, Embracing Brokenness Ministries
Host, *Embracing Brokenness Podcast*

In the craziness of life there are times we forget why God put us here. We lose some drive. Forget the goal. Grow complacent. *Checking the Boxes Only You Can Check* reminds us of the kind of person God created us to be—and how to get there.

—*Tim Shoemaker*
National speaker
Author of over 20 books including *The Very Best, Hands-On, Kinda Dangerous Family Devotions*

Who wants to show up in heaven with a long list of unchecked boxes? I don't! That's why I'm grateful for Jay Payleitner's latest book. He's opened my eyes to unchecked boxes that—in Christ—I really can check. Just maybe, I can do my part to have a life-changing impact on my corner of the world.

—*Jon Gauger*
Moody Radio host
Author of *Kids Say the Wisest Things*

CHECKING THE BOXES ONLY YOU CAN CHECK

40 Ways to Make the World a Better Place

JAY PAYLEITNER

WHITAKER
HOUSE

CHECKING THE BOXES ONLY YOU CAN CHECK
40 Ways to Make the World a Better Place

jaypayleitner.com

ISBN: 979-8-88769-227-2
eBook ISBN: 979-8-88769-228-9
Printed in the United States of America
© 2024 by Jay Payleitner

Whitaker House
1030 Hunt Valley Circle
New Kensington, PA 15068
www.whitakerhouse.com

LC record available at https://lccn.loc.gov/2024005209
LC ebook record available at https://lccn.loc.gov/2024005210

1 2 3 4 5 6 7 8 9 10 11 ⬛ 31 30 29 28 27 26 25 24

PROLOGUE

Today's mainstream culture trashes Christians. They claim we're narrow-minded, hate-filled, and don't care about the world. But you and I know that's just not true.

So how do we flip that script?

As it turns out, God has placed different assignments and quests in front of each one of us. We each get a chance to choose which boxes to check.

It's time to recognize our purpose. To model love. To connect the generations. To defy the lions. To feed the enemy. To throw starfish. And to make the world a better place.

In other words, what if Christians started acting like Christians?

CONTENTS

Being a Christian is less about cautiously avoiding sin than about courageously and actively doing God's will.[1]
—Eric Metaxas

The greatest single cause of atheism in the world today is Christians who acknowledge Jesus with their lips and walk out the door and deny Him by their lifestyle. That is what an unbelieving world simply finds unbelievable.[2]
—Brennan Manning

Each one should test their own actions. Then they can take pride in themselves alone, without comparing themselves to someone else, for each one should carry their own load.
—Galatians 6:4–5

1. Eric Metaxas, *Bonhoeffer: Pastor, Martyr, Prophet, Spy* (Nashville, TN: Thomas Nelson, 2010), 486.
2. Marcus Yoars, "'Ragamuffin Gospel' Author Brennan Manning Dies," *Charisma News*, April 13, 2013, https://www.charismanews.com/us/39076-ragamuffin-author-brennan-manning-dies.

FOREWORD

As a teenager, I desperately wanted to know the answers to these questions: "Who am I? Why am I here? Where am I going?" At the time, I thought asking those questions was unique to me.

I sought answers at home, in my community, at church, at university, and through the acquisition of power and prestige, but I ultimately found those answers to be meaningless.

My dedicated quest finally led to two life-changing revelations. One: everyone is asking those same questions. Two: the answer is Jesus.

Decades later, those same two revelations continue to drive my relationships, my work, and the entire Josh McDowell Ministry. The world is searching for answers, and we are committed to sharing the truth of the gospel with enthusiasm, boldness, creativity, and courage.

I'm humbled to say that thousands of staff and volunteers have joined in that mission. Early on, I realized that recruiting a wide variety of passionate believers was critical because every individual brings different gifts and a different calling.

We all ask those three questions: *Who am I? Why am I here? Where am I going?* In many ways, the answers are the same for every follower of Christ: I am a child of God. I'm here to give glory to the Creator. I'm heaven bound and working to take as many people with me as possible.

However, when doing a self-assessment on how to apply our personal gifts and calling, those same three questions prove to be valuable in a completely different capacity. God gives each of us a distinctive personality, unique purpose, and customized life path.

In other words, we all have different boxes to check!

As a matter of fact, God promises to assign you specific tasks you dare not miss, because those are boxes *only you can check*: "*In Christ we, though many, form one body, and each member belongs to all the others. We have different gifts, according to the grace given to each of us*" (Romans 12:5–6).

My life is testimony to the fact that identifying and checking the boxes chosen just for you brings a sense of fulfillment found nowhere else, and I pray you also experience that firsthand. But, much more than that, I can confirm that when you access your personal giftedness, you fulfill your destiny as a follower of Christ made in the image of God.

When that happens, I promise, your life itself will shine light in the darkness and serve as an answer to the questions being asked by everyone you meet.

—Josh McDowell
International speaker, apologist, and author/coauthor of more than 140 books, including *More Than a Carpenter* and *Evidence That Demands a Verdict*

INTRODUCTION

"There's a responsibility in being a person. It's more than just taking up space where air would be."[3]
—John Steinbeck

This world as we know it is worth celebrating and protecting. How can we not appreciate the wonder of creation? The intricacies of a spider's web. The grandeur of a thundering waterfall. A galloping horse. A bouncing puppy. A humpback whale breaching the surface of the sea. The promise of a sunrise. The depth of the night sky.

The human condition can also reflect the best of this world. A child's laughter. A newlywed couple sharing hopes and dreams. A grandchild running through the front door calling out for Grandma or Grandpa. The creativity and devotion of artists, composers, writers, athletes, and inventors. Our own ability to work, play, imagine, and strive for excellence.

The world provides so much for which to be grateful.

At the same time, most of us are crushed and confused by how brutality, negligence, and hostility seem to be on the increase. Wars. Terrorism. Mass shootings. Racism. Hate speech. Extreme

---

3. John Steinbeck, *East of Eden* (United States: Viking Press, 1952; New York: Penguin Books, 1979), 346. Citation to the Penguin edition. https://archive.org/details/east-of-eden_202007.

poverty. Child abuse. Teen depression. Bullying. Environmental disasters. Pornography. Genocide. Suicide.

Something has to change. Right?

As someone who believes in a creator God who brings order out of chaos, you may find yourself wondering, "What should be my response to the turmoil and strife? How can I make the world a better place? What is my God-given responsibility?"

These are excellent questions. No doubt they leave you feeling curious, confused, empowered, humbled, and eager—all at the same time!

If we begin at the beginning, we are already aware of the first two assignments God gave to Adam and Eve.

So God created mankind in his own image, in the image of God he created them; male and female he created them. God blessed them and said to them, "Be fruitful and increase in number; fill the earth and subdue it." (Genesis 1:27–28)

The LORD God took the man and put him in the Garden of Eden to work it and take care of it. (Genesis 2:15)

These clear mandates tell us that humanity needs to do more than simply exist in this world. Made in God's image, we are called to nurture and protect it. To be stewards. And to raise children who do the same.

We should not be surprised that the opening chapters of the Bible have given us an assignment. All of humankind is to "subdue" the earth and "take care of" it.

While the above passages describe the big-picture view of God's assignment, they don't give specific instructions to specific individuals. Just look around at your own circle of friends and family members, and you'll realize that we all have different gifts and abilities. That tells us that even if we're all aiming at the same destination, each of us still has our own set of assignments.

Some assignments are collaborative efforts, while others require a solo attack. Some tasks need to be accomplished once, while others turn out to be daily (or ongoing) responsibilities. Some are universal obligations for all eight billion of us on earth. Some tasks have been assigned to you alone at this specific time and place.

So, what are those boxes that only you can check? What are the ways you can make the world a better place?

In his letter to the Galatians, Paul offers this guidance:

Each one should test their own actions. Then they can take pride in themselves alone, without comparing themselves to someone else, for each one should carry their own load.
(Galatians 6:4–5)

Did this passage surprise you? Read it again.

Are you seeing any principles that challenge any long-held beliefs or understandings? For example, should we test or trust? Should we be proud of our accomplishments, or does "pride go before destruction"? (See Proverbs 16:18.) If we're not supposed to compare ourselves to others, what's the value of mentoring or modeling how to live? Finally, doesn't Galatians 6:2 tell us to *"carry each other's burdens"*?

If you're scratching your head, that's a good thing. God wants us to think deeply about every verse of Scripture in order to better apply it to our lives. Feel free at any time to put this book down and do a deep dive into any Bible passage you come across.

In any case, you'll want to keep moving your bookmark in these pages. These chapters deliver a forty-point plan for checking the right boxes and thereby changing our world. You won't find any political posturing, shame-inducing guilt, or finger-pointing. Instead, these short chapters lay out a plan devised centuries ago by the Creator Himself. That strategy includes the best course of action for the earth and each one of its inhabitants—including you!

In addition, here's an unsettling thought: The world is watching anyone who call themselves a Christian. How we respond to the crises of today will either draw naysayers and fence-sitters to join our ranks or will entrench the evildoers more deeply into their dark void.

So, here's your challenge. Read, ponder, and engage in these forty objectives—perhaps one per day for the next six weeks—and then literally expect unmistakable transformation.

With each box you check, check your own spirit. Keep a journal. Anticipate an attitude shift among your neighbors, family members, and friends. Even watch the news headlines, both local and around the world. Your commitment to making the world a better place will make a difference.

Keep your favorite writing utensil handy, and get ready to check off at least a few of these boxes, metaphorical or otherwise.

Thanks for blazing this ancient trail anew.

1

WORK HARD

"I am a great believer in luck.
The harder I work, the more of it I seem to have."[4]
—Coleman Cox

Sorry to begin this book with such disappointing news. But, of course, there's work to be done. And that should not come as a surprise.

You may have been hoping these forty chapters would reveal forty heavenly secrets to breezing through life, saving the planet and all its inhabitants without breaking a sweat; but that's not how God designed things. It turns out that leaving this world better than we found it requires the thoughtful pursuit of actual effort. In other words, thinking and doing.

The fact you've opened this book suggests you're willing to participate in that two-part exercise. Planning and working. Discerning God's will and putting your nose to the grindstone.

The case can be made that planning carefully is even more important than doing the work itself. The last thing any committed worker wants to do is dig the hole in the wrong place, paint the house the wrong color, write the speech on the wrong topic, or fly the plane to the wrong airport. You should never feel like it's a

---

4. Coleman Cox, *Listen to This* (San Francisco: Coleman Cox Publishing, 1922), vii. https://www.google.com/books/edition/Listen_to_this/bNUlAQAAMAAJ?hl=en&gbpv=1.

waste of time to pause and ask yourself, "Is this the right thing to do?" or "Will my efforts honor God?"

Still, let's dedicate the remainder of this opening chapter to the value of work.

THE NATURE AND VALUE OF WORK

According to a physicist, work can be defined as "the transfer of energy by a force acting on an object as it is displaced."[5] In other words, work means moving something from here to there. Examples might be kicking a can down the street, mashing buttons on a gaming controller, or relocating yourself from the sofa to the front door to retrieve a DoorDash delivery.

Those examples of "work" might help you pass a physics quiz. But they also demonstrate that, although we can trust science, we can't always trust every scientist.

If we really want to check a box that's worth checking, then our work should probably be less self-centered and more meaningful, productive, and altruistic. Adding the idea of working "hard" suggests our work should actually take us out of our comfort zone. Toil, training, skill, exertion, fortitude, creativity, and even courage are words that come to mind. Can you relate?

In God's economy, there's dignity and virtue in work. Armed with a solid work ethic and the ability to finish a task, you'll be rewarded with projects fit for a king. Or, at least, you'll get a chance to hang out in the throne room. The Bible says, *"Do you see a person skilled in his work? He will stand before kings"* (Proverbs 22:29 NASB).

For some, the prospect of getting recognized by royalty will inspire you to invest your heart, soul, blood, sweat, and tears in work that matters. On the other hand, maybe you are motivated by simpler goals, like having food on your plate. Second

5. LibreTexts, "6.2: Work-The Scientific Definition," (OpenStax), https://phys.libretexts. org/Courses/Tuskegee_University/Algebra_Based_Physics_I/06%3A_Work_Energy_ and_Energy_Resources/6.02%3A_Work-_The_Scientific_Definition.

Thessalonians 3:10 clearly states, *"The one who is unwilling to work shall not eat."* Stated in a more positive way, Proverbs 12:11 (NLT) promises, *"A hard worker has plenty of food."*

To confirm, the Bible indicates hard work will gain you honor and sustenance. Both are commendable rewards. Still, the fundamental question we will be asking in these chapters before any boxes are checked is this: "How does that activity make the world a better place?"

GOOD WORK IMPROVES YOUR ATTITUDE

The Bible tells us that finding fulfillment in your work is a gift from God that makes you happier and promotes benevolence. *"I know that there is nothing better for people than to be happy and to do good while they live. That each of them may eat and drink, and find satisfaction in all their toil—this is the gift of God"* (Ecclesiastes 3:12–13).

COMMITTED WORK SHARPENS YOUR INTEGRITY

By earning your keep, you become a model for those around you and avoid adding a burden or being a hardship on others. *"For you yourselves know how you ought to follow our example. We were not idle when we were with you, nor did we eat anyone's food without paying for it. On the contrary, we worked night and day, laboring and toiling so that we would not be a burden to any of you"* (2 Thessalonians 3:7–8).

WORTHWHILE WORK SETS AN EXAMPLE AND DEFLECTS NAYSAYERS

By working hard, you'll gain respect from friends, students, clients, bosses, and even enemies. *"Show yourself in all respects to be a model of good works, and in your teaching show integrity, dignity, and sound speech that cannot be condemned, so that an opponent may be put to shame, having nothing evil to say about us"* (Titus 2:7–8 ESV).

HONEST WORK CAN TURN YOUR LIFE AROUND AND BE A BLESSING TO OTHERS

Work can be life-changing, even for rebels and scalawags, as well as for those whose lives they touch. *"Let the thief no longer steal, but rather let him labor, doing honest work with his own hands, so that he may have something to share with anyone in need"* (Ephesians 4:28 ESV).

So then—for both personal rewards and benefits beyond your own self-interest—let's get to work.

☑ CHECKING THE BOX

For sure, hard work makes you a better person. But I hope you see how your improved attitude, inspiring lifestyle, and increasing generosity can have a positive impact on family, friends, colleagues, and even people you may never meet. Future chapters will have more content on choosing, planning, prioritizing, and even disengaging from work. For now, let's agree that the work of an individual—such as yourself—can literally make one corner of the world a better place.

TO PONDER OR SHARE...

☐ 1. What was your first job?

☐ 2. Describe what you consider to be one of your most fulfilling days at work.

☐ 3. How do you respond to coworkers or co-laborers who don't pull their weight?

☐ 4. Have you ever developed a new friendship with a work colleague, vendor, or client because of how well you worked with that person?

☐ 5. Should work be hard?

2

STOP MAKING EXCUSES

*"The man who is good at making an excuse is
seldom good at anything else."*[6]
—Benjamin Franklin, attributed

After chapter one put you to work, you may be hoping chapter
two lets you off the hook. Sorry, no such luck.

One of the great failures of today's culture is that no one wants
to take responsibility for their actions. Excuses are served up rou-
tinely, and they often include unappealing side dishes of whining,
protesting, and blame shifting.

Making excuses is as old as history itself and was pivotal to
the sequence of events surrounding the first sin. Remember Adam
in the garden of Eden? (See Genesis 3.) His new bride offered
him fruit from the one tree that had been expressly designated as
off-limits. Without much thought, the appointed caretaker of the
entire world took a big ol' bite. When confronted by the Creator,
the first man delivered the first pathetic excuse. Adam attempted
to incriminate both God and Eve with one short phrase, by blaming *"the woman you put here with me"* (Genesis 3:12).

The first couple disobeyed God and then lied to God, but
I think it was the whining and blame shifting that put the final

6. D. Akenhead and Sons, *Liber Facetiarum: Being a Collection of Curious and Interesting Anecdotes* (Newcastle Upon Tyne, England: D. Akenhead and Sons, 1809), 182. https://babel.hathitrust.org/cgi/pt?id=nyp.33433074922000&seq=204.

nail in their coffin. Adam and Eve were not alone in their excuse making. Other examples of whine-filled excuses from Scripture are easy to find.

Moses had an extended conversation with God speaking through a burning bush. (See Exodus 3.) After receiving specific instructions to lead the Israelites out of Egypt, Moses came up with all kinds of excuses that sounded like the whining of a petulant teenager. "Why me?" "What should I say?" "What if they don't believe me?" "I don't talk so good." "Can't You send someone else?" (See Exodus 4.)

Still, whiners, take note: It is possible to undergo a proactive and positive attitude adjustment. With God's help, Moses stopped making excuses and became the leader and hero of the Jewish people.

Proverbs 22:13 offers a justifiable excuse that may prove valuable, especially if it applies to your particular situation: "*The sluggard says, 'There's a lion outside! I'll be killed in the public square!'*" But for most of us, there is no lion lounging in our front yard, which means using that excuse pretty much proves you are, indeed, a good-for-nothing sluggard.

In the parable of the talents, two investors earned a profit on an investment provided by their master. But the third man didn't want to risk losing the money and let fear be his excuse. He blame shifted to the master, saying, "*I knew that you are a hard man, harvesting where you have not sown and gathering where you have not scattered seed. So I was afraid and went out and hid your gold in the ground. See, here is what belongs to you*" (Matthew 25:24–25). A few verses later, we read how that unimaginative excuse maker is tossed into the darkness, weeping, and gnashing his teeth. (See verse 30.)

All that to say, dodging accountability increases the odds your own sad carcass will wind up wailing in the darkness, while accepting personal responsibility opens your ears to hearing God's plan and may even pave the way for financial prosperity. It's easy to see how being whine free is a worthy box to check for you as an individual. But how does it make the world a better place?

THE BENEFITS OF MINIMIZED WHINING

LESS WHINING REDUCES NOISE POLLUTION

No one likes a whiner or their whining. Consider fictional characters you may recognize for their extreme whining, such as Ron Weasley, Screech, Daffy Duck, Anakin Skywalker, Grandpa Joad, Eeyore, Scarlett O'Hara, the Cowardly Lion, and Holden Caufield. Aren't you relieved when they finally exit the scene you're watching or the passage you're reading? For the same reason, successful professional athletes learn to accept blown calls as part of the game while lesser athletes make excuses, gripe about being benched, and justifiably get cut from the team.

WHINING DRAGS DOWN YOUR ENTIRE TRIBE

In Numbers chapters 13 and 14, we read how Moses sent a dozen men to scout the promised land. Reporting back, they expressed fear and hopelessness, an attitude that quickly spread among the people. *"All the Israelites grumbled against Moses and Aaron, and the whole assembly said to them, 'If only we had died in Egypt! Or in this wilderness!'"* (Numbers 14:2). That grumbling leads to rebellion, which leads to God's punishment. Which leads to the greatest fear of the Israelites coming true, as only two adults who had left Egypt some forty years earlier, Caleb and Joshua, would enter the promised land. The rest, who had chosen whining over trusting God, died in the desert.

MAKING EXCUSES FORESTALLS CREATIVE SOLUTIONS

The classic excuse "The dog ate my homework" is not fooling anyone. Except yourself. Often it takes more creative energy to come up with a lame excuse than to work on solving the problem. You may not know their names, but Roberta Lawson and Mary

McLaren, Josephine Cochrane, and Mary Anderson chose *not* to whine about messy tea leaves, dirty dishes, or driving in the rain. Instead, they identified a problem and invented the tea bag, dishwasher, and windshield wiper.

ACCEPTING RESPONSIBILITY GAINS RESPECT

Grumbling less while striving for greater productivity earns admiration from others, reflects your humble faith, and may even open the door to sincere conversations on what's really important. *"Make it your goal to live a quiet life, minding your own business and working with your hands, just as we instructed you before. Then people who are not believers will respect the way you live, and you will not need to depend on others"* (1 Thessalonians 4:11–12 NLT).

Whether you're a leader, innovator, technician, or artist, when you find yourself making excuses—or having to listen to the excuses of others—you'll almost always find your productivity and influence also grinding to a halt.

☑ CHECKING THE BOX

> The world works best when humanity is looking for answers, not pointing fingers or passing the buck. When we look for something or someone to blame, negativity flows out from the heart, mind, and spirit. Yes, we need to identify the source of any failure or miscalculation. But effective problem-solving requires that we move from assigning blame to accepting responsibility.

TO PONDER OR SHARE...

☐ 1. When confronted with an unpleasant task, what's your go-to excuse?

☐ 2. Which of the whining fictional characters on the previous page do you identify with the most? Which one makes you cringe the most?

☐ 3. Do you tend to grumble more at the beginning of a difficult task or as you near the end? (In Exodus, the Israelites did both!)

☐ 4. When is it okay to whine and/or make excuses? What's the best alternative to whining?

☐ 5. When are you most likely to blame God for your circumstances?

3

GO ABOVE AND BEYOND

*"We are going to relentlessly chase perfection, knowing full
well we will not catch it, because nothing is perfect.
But we are going to relentlessly chase it, because in the process
we will catch excellence. "[7]*
—Vince Lombardi

To summarize the first two chapters: Work hard and take responsibility. Check and check. But maybe don't stop there. Let's consider the concept of *excellence.*

Hard work may or may not lead to excellence. Certainly, sweat, and sustained effort increase the odds of success in any chosen endeavor, but the more ambitious goal of excellence refers to a level of achievement beyond merely getting the job done.

In a similar fashion, when you eliminate excuses, you increase your chances of seeing a task through to the end. That's almost always a worthy goal. But delivering excellence requires more than merely taking personal responsibility.

Excellence is about exceeding expectations. It's about surprising yourself and others by what you can achieve.

Notable characters in the Bible give us a glimpse of what it takes to be excellent. In the Old Testament book of Daniel, we

7. Chuck Carlson, *Game of My Life: 25 Stories of Packers Football* (Sports Publishing LLC, 2004), 149.

read that King Darius saw how *"Daniel so distinguished himself among the administrators and the satraps by his exceptional qualities that the king planned to set him over the whole kingdom"* (Daniel 6:3). Rooted in his faithfulness to God, Daniel would interpret visions, stand by his convictions, and survive the lions' den.

During some of Israel's darkest days, Ruth demonstrated excellence in her loyalty to her mother-in-law, Naomi, saying, *"Your people will be my people and your God my God"* (Ruth 1:16). Ruth's diligence while gleaning in the fields gained the attention of the heroic figure Boaz. (See Ruth 2.) Ruth's reputation spread due to pursuing the right things in the right way for the right reason. Ruth and Boaz eventually married and would go on to be the grandparents of David.

When Jesus performed His first miracle by changing water to wine at the wedding at Cana, He confirmed that, when presented with any challenge, He doesn't settle for mediocrity. He brings out the best, sometimes even saving the best for last. You may recall that the master of the banquet said, *"You have saved the best till now"* (John 2:10).

In today's world, excellent work continues to be a testimony to Christ. Chick-fil-A, to name a familiar example, is transparent about the connection between their commitment to exceptional service and their corporate purpose "to glorify God by being a faithful steward of all that is entrusted to us."[8]

Other notable companies demonstrate that excellence, earning a fair profit, and extolling Christian virtues go hand in hand. John Deere refused to repossess farm equipment during the Great Depression.[9] In-N-Out Burger prints subtle Bible references on

---

8. "What is Chick-fil-A's corporate purpose?" Chick-fil-A, https://www.chick-fil-a.com/customer-support/who-we-are/our-culture-and-values/what-is-chick-fil-as-corporate-purpose.

9. "John Deere Heritage Runs Deep for Many Americans," MachineFinder, February 8, 2012, https://www.machinefinder.com/ww/en-US/articles/john-deere-heritage-runs-deep-for-many-americans-2000.

their paper cups, fry boats, and burger wrappers.[10] Tyson Foods employs over a hundred chaplains who provide pastoral care, transportation, housing, and other needs to employees and their families in more than twenty states.[11]

Excellence can also be found in the work of scores of organizations founded on Christian principles, including the Salvation Army, Prison Fellowship, St. Jude Children's Research Hospital, the Mayo Clinic, Johns Hopkins Hospital, Habitat for Humanity, World Relief, Compassion International, Leprosy Mission International, Food for the Poor, Alcoholics Anonymous, and Amnesty International. Schools like Harvard, Yale, Princeton, Cambridge, and Oxford also flourished in their early years because of their Christian roots.

Lest we forget, biblical provenance inspired the world-changing work of Handel, Bach, Mozart, Beethoven, Stravinsky, Schubert, Michelangelo, Raphael, Rembrandt, da Vinci, Galileo, Kepler, Isaac Newton, Marconi, George Washington Carver, Jane Addams, Clara Barton, Lech Walesa, Louis Braille, Dr. Martin Luther King Jr., and tens of thousands of doctors and medical professionals who travel to minister to the poorest of the poor every year on medical mission trips.

Such work should inspire all of us to strive for excellence. Don't check that box for your own sake; do so to give glory to God and make the world a better place.

KEY ATTRIBUTES OF EXCELLENCE

EXCELLENCE SETS A HIGH STANDARD

At the end of each day recorded in the opening chapter of Genesis, God looked at creation and *"saw that it was good"* (Genesis

---

10. Alix Martichoux, "Which Bible verses are printed on In-N-Out's burgers, fries and milkshakes?" KTLA.com, September 18, 2022, https://ktla.com/news/which-bible-verses-are-printed-on-in-n-outs-burgers-fries-and-milkshakes/.

11. Tithe.ly, "7 Christian Companies That Inspire Us Now," Tithe.ly, November 9, 2023, https://get.tithe.ly/blog/7-christian-companies-that-inspire-us-now.

1:10). Our work could never compare to God's work, but the standard has been set.

EXCELLENCE PROVES THE VALUE OF COLLABORATION

It's a rare inventor or scientist who works solo. Most pioneers will affirm how their achievements were possible only because they were working with a great team or standing on the shoulders of those who had gone before. Giving credit doesn't diminish your achievement; it validates your reputation and the broad impact of your work.

EXCELLENCE BEGINS WITH ATTITUDE

Excellence isn't just about a finished product; it's about exhibiting integrity in the process. When we cut corners, skip steps, or look for a quick fix, quality suffers. Buildings collapse, reputations are damaged, and lawyers gleefully get involved.

EXCELLENCE INSPIRES ENTHUSIASM

Some people may see an achievement and think, "I could never do that." But, more often, being witness to an inspired achievement leads to curiosity, fascination, and a desire to be part of something bigger than yourself. Excellence begets excellence.

EXCELLENCE DOES NOT EQUAL PERFECTION

If you've been given an extraordinary vision for the next season of your life, you may hesitate, thinking, "It's impossible, so why bother?" Please don't sell yourself short. Instead, apply your best self to the challenge—with the right attitude and in collaboration with others—and don't be surprised if the result turns out to be pretty darn close to perfection.

The great inventors, artists, builders, and humanitarians of history somehow caught a clear revelation before they could do what they did. Noah trusted God's plan before building the ark. Moses had no travel brochures, but he did envision the promised land. In Acts 10, Peter had a vision of sharing the gospel with Gentiles. With that in mind, your first step toward excellence is to open your heart and mind to the possibility of gaining a glimpse of God's plan for your life.

☑ CHECKING THE BOX

Shoot for excellence and you may even get a smidgen of fame thrown in. The dozens of examples of excellent work listed above made history and led to worldwide recognition and fame. That's not necessarily a bad thing, but it really shouldn't be the goal. There are more important priorities. Famously, Jesus said, *"What good is it for someone to gain the whole world, yet forfeit their soul?"* (Mark 8:36).

TO PONDER OR SHARE...

☐ 1. Think of a time when you performed with excellence, even surprising yourself.

☐ 2. Of the people in your circle of influence, with whom could you partner on your quest for excellence?

☐ 3. Do you know someone who does great work? Let them know this week what you think of their efforts.

☐ 4. Have you ever made excellence a goal and fallen way short? How did you respond?

☐ 5. If this chapter inspired you to shoot for excellence, what's your true motivation?

4

EXPECT SILVER LININGS

"Life will never grow dull so long as you joyously greet every obstacle as an opportunity."[12]
—Newton Newkirk

No one will ever accuse me of being all sunshine and roses. I figure that's a good thing. After all, crud happens. Clouds will roll in. Weeds will grow. Mistakes will be made. Sometimes the bad guys win. What's more, there's something suspicious about that person who is a perpetual ray of sunshine.

Nonetheless, history honors a slew of optimists who should be celebrated for overcoming challenges and bringing a surprising positivity to difficult circumstances. Anne Frank held on to hope for a brighter future even as she hid in an attic from the Nazis for two years. As expressed in her testimony, "I don't think about all the misery, but about the beauty that still remains."[13]

Thomas Edison famously displayed audacious optimism in his goal of engineering a practical light bulb. The visionary inventor is commonly quoted as having said, "I have not failed. I've just found 10,000 ways that won't work."

12. Newton Newkirk, "All Sorts by Newton Newkirk, What the Sphinx Says," *The Boston Post*, November 14, 1918, 14. https://www.newspapers.com/image/71793092/?terms=.
13. Anne Frank, *The Diary of a Young Girl: The Definitive Edition*, ed. Otto H. Frank and Mirjam Pressler, trans. Susan Massotty (New York: Doubleday, 1995), 157, https://archive.org/details/AnneFrankTheDiaryOfAYoungGirl_201606/mode/2up?view=theater.

Nelson Mandela somehow emerged from twenty-seven years in a South African prison with a forgiving heart and a sense of humor. The internationally esteemed Nobel Prize winner would often catch a new acquaintance off guard by saying, "I am so honored to meet you." While those kinds of self-deprecating remarks charmed audiences, it was his ability to find silver linings that may have been his greatest legacy. He said, "I never lose. I either win or learn."

Assessing the true heart of historical figures is a tricky business. But there seems to be significant value in the idea of facing adversity with hope and envisioning a silver lining even in the darkest clouds.

One strategy for learning that skill is to look back. Surely you have endured a setback or calamity that felt like the end of the world but in the end left you stronger, wiser, and better off. Personally, I've seen this happen time and again. My most obvious silver lining came after being fired from a lucrative career as a copywriter on Michigan Avenue in Chicago. During that season in major market advertising, I saw it as my fantasy job and God-given destiny. Lucky for me, a new creative director came in and cleaned house, which led directly to my career in Christian media. Unexpectedly life-changing.

An obvious example from the Bible comes from the life of Joseph. Genesis chapters thirty-seven through forty-one record how he was sold into slavery by his jealous brothers, tempted and then framed by Potiphar's wife, and imprisoned for years. Still, rather than bemoaning his fate, Joseph somehow found opportunity in each setback and rose in power and stature. His integrity and optimism would save Egypt (and his family) from famine and be a lasting model of the power of forgiveness.

The bigger point is that whatever you're going through, God can and will use it for good so that your life can bring Him glory. Romans 8:28 confirms, *"We know that in all things God works for* the good of those who love him, who have been called according to his purpose."

Anyone who commits to emulating Joseph can start to expect silver linings even on their darkest days. Soon you'll be able to look back and see a long trail of surprising U-turns as today's crud turns to tomorrow's gold. When you check that box, the world becomes a better place because you refused to believe hope was in short supply.

FROM ADVERSITY TO TRIUMPH WITH HOPE AND OPTIMISM

ANTICIPATING A SILVER LINING CAN HELP CREATE THE SILVER LINING

You'll never find an answer when you're looking down with your hands in your pockets and feeling sorry for yourself. But when you know there's a light, you'll keep reaching until you find the light switch. Knowing God will protect and provide for us should embolden each of us to be part of the solution: *"God will meet all your needs according to the riches of his glory in Christ Jesus"* (Philippians 4:19).

OPTIMISM PROVES THE NAYSAYERS WRONG

During the COVID-19 lockdown, way too many people seemed to enjoy pointing fingers and feeling sorry for themselves. Others saw the lockdown as an opportunity to connect with family, enjoy virtual calls with new friends across the world, write that book or screenplay, or master a new activity. What a difference.

DISASTERS BOND COMMUNITIES

Natural and man-made disasters can actually bring out the best in people. Consider the human response to hurricanes, earthquakes, wildfires, terrorism, war, civil disobedience, and so on. Because of the fallen nature of humanity, catastrophes may precipitate an increase in looting, fake charities, phishing schemes, insurance fraud, and other heartbreaking developments. But the opposite is more likely and more impressive. Strangers help strangers. Truckloads of supplies roll in from across the country. People line up at the Red Cross to donate blood. And volunteers come together to provide shelter for their communities and shoulders to lean on. It's like Mister Rogers would say to kids watching scary news stories: "Look for the helpers. You will always find people who are helping."

HOPE GOES HAND IN HAND WITH LOVE

Love is a feeling, commitment, and connection. It's also a verb. Love is something we do. The "love passage" in the Bible finishes this way: "[Love] *always protects, always trusts, always hopes, always perseveres. Love never fails*" (1 Corinthians 13:7–8).

It's fairly easy to see that being hopeful helps you not only expect a silver lining but also be the catalyst that triggers an outpouring of solutions and remedies for yourself, your loved ones, strangers, and the world.

☑ CHECKING THE BOX

This short chapter may seem like it's denying that illness and catastrophes can bring destruction, death, pain, and heartache. Actually, it's the opposite. Let's all agree that life is not all sunshine and roses. When we find ourselves in the midst of tragedy, we need to ask questions like: "How should I respond?" "Where is God working?" "How can I use my gifts and resources to alleviate suffering or bring hope to my fellow humans?"

TO PONDER OR SHARE...

☐ 1. Are you a glass half-empty or glass half-full kind of person?

☐ 2. Who are your personal heroes? Do they have a sense of optimism?

☐ 3. How can setbacks be a good thing?

☐ 4. Do you tend to be one of "the helpers" referenced by Mister Rogers? Or are you too busy looking for scapegoats, pitfalls, and excuses?

☐ 5. When have you experienced Romans 8:28 to be true in your own life? Memorize that verse!

5

HARVEST YOUR GIFTS

*"Our gifts and talents should also be turned over to Him.
They should be recognized for what they are, God's loan to
us, and should never be considered in any sense our own."*[14]
—A. W. Tozer

When our son Randy was in kindergarten, he told my wife
he wanted to be Superman for Halloween. That was an easy yes.
One of Rita's many talents is her ability to visualize a garment or
stuffed animal, lay out a pattern, and spend less time than you can
imagine finishing a project at her sewing machine.

Early in October, mother and son went to the sewing store
to buy blue, red, and yellow fabric and look for just the right
Butterick sewing pattern. They discovered that superhero pack-
ets from Butterick offered two surprises: iron-on logos officially
trademarked by DC Comics and patterns sized for both kids
and adults. Illustrations on the cover of the packet even showed a
father and son posed valiantly side by side.

Rita was inspired, and Randy was thrilled to be in on the
secret. Without any forewarning, my talented and sneaky wife
bought enough fabric to make two costumes: one for Randy and

---

14. A. W. Tozer, *The Pursuit of God* (Harrisburg, PA: Christian Publications, Inc., 1948),
28.

one for his dad. With a cheeky smile, she presented the costume to me on the morning of October 31.

Of course, I didn't have any choice but to go along with the plan. My then-muscular physique filled out the costume quite nicely. I made a rollicking guest appearance at Randy's kindergarten class and famously trick-or-treated with him around the neighborhood. Rita watched self-effacingly from a distance, knowing she had instigated the whole memory-making experience.[15]

Here's the point: Rita used one of her gifts that she had developed years before to time-stamp a memory for her son and husband. It was a gift that unmistakably made our world (including our neighborhood and local elementary school) a better place.

Make sense? At this point, your mind should be identifying and cataloging your own gifts and abilities with the intent of using them for the benefit of others. Not to bring yourself glory, but to give a smile, bring hope, feed, clothe, rescue, soothe, or bring salvation to a friend, loved one, enemy, or stranger.

Need other specific real-life examples? Consider these: Barnabas's gift of encouragement (see Acts 4:36–37), Noah's obedience (see Genesis 6:22), Job's perseverance and faith (see James 5:11), Nehemiah's leadership and organizational skills to rebuild the walls of Jerusalem (see Nehemiah 6:15–16), Lydia's gift of hospitality to Paul and Silas (see Acts 16:14–15, 40), and, finally—without the aid of a sewing machine—Tabitha (aka Dorcas) making tunics and other clothing for the poor (see Acts 9:36–41).

There is a popular saying that goes, "The meaning of life is to find your gift. The purpose of life is to give it away." Most people miss this, but doesn't it sound like an obvious box to check? We're talking about gifts and talents you *already* possess that can impact the lives of real people in your close circle of influence and around the world.

15. Adapted from Jay Payleitner, *Moms Bringing Out the Best in Dads* (Eugene, OR: Harvest House Publishers, 2022), 70–71.

HOW TO USE YOUR GIFTS

USE YOUR GIFTS TO INSPIRE

Writers use words. Sculptors fashion stone or clay. Composers create music. Architects erect buildings. Chefs delight tastebuds. And a gifted seamstress can bring joy to a kindergartener, surprise a young father, make aprons for soup kitchen volunteers, or inspire confidence in a young woman who can't afford a dress for her senior prom.

USE YOUR GIFTS TO TEACH AND MENTOR

You may have no desire to speak to an auditorium full of strangers. But you can certainly invite a curious young person to join you at a workbench, kitchen counter, backyard garden, art easel, batting cage, workstation, or sewing machine for lessons that will last a lifetime.

USE YOUR VOICE TO SHARE YOUR BEST INSIGHT

How did you acquire and master the personal skills that have come to mind as you've read this chapter? Some came easy. Some you learned the hard way. Share your journey of discovery on a podcast, in a book, in a classroom, or at a workshop through your library, park district, or community outreach program.

ASK THOSE YOU TRUST TO IDENTIFY YOUR GIFTS

Many people who have a servant's heart and live in humility may not even realize the amazing gifts they've been given. It's quite possible you've received many undiscovered blessings God wants you to share. Find the courage to ask a few friends or loved ones to honestly assess the gifts and skills you might be able to give back to the world. Prepare your heart and mind for a revealing brainstorming session.

Consider how the apostle Peter challenged us to live for God:

Each of you should use whatever gift you have received to serve others, as faithful stewards of God's grace in its various forms. If anyone speaks, they should do so as one who speaks the very words of God. If anyone serves, they should do so with the strength God provides, so that in all things God may be praised through Jesus Christ. To him be the glory and the power for ever and ever. Amen. (1 Peter 4:10–11)

☑ CHECKING THE BOX

There is no one else on the planet like you. No one with your circle of influence. With your life experience. With your exact gifts and skills on loan to you from your Creator. As we established in chapter one, you don't just have work to do—your work has purpose. Open your heart and mind to the possibilities within your reach this very day. Many of those opportunities are calling your name. Oh, yeah—and if you're a seamstress and happen to know a dad and son who need a laugh, feel free to steal Rita's inspired idea this October.

TO PONDER OR SHARE...

☐ 1. Have you ever been the surprised recipient of someone's giftedness?

☐ 2. Who knows you well enough to honestly and enthusiastically help you identify your gifts?

☐ 3. Which gifts were you born with? Which of your gifts are from the Holy Spirit?

☐ 4. Is it okay to earn an income from using your gifts to serve others and give glory to God?

☐ 5. Who do you know that is shy or reluctant to use their gifts? How can you encourage and inspire them?

6

ESTEEM WILDLIFE

"The greatest threat to our planet is the belief that someone else will save it."[16]
—Robert Swan

When I was a kid, we always brought a bag of marshmallows when we visited Brookfield Zoo just outside Chicago. Back then, it was common practice—even encouraged by zookeepers—to toss marshmallows through the fence to the eager polar bears who sometimes caught the sweet treats in their mouth. The crowd loved it. The bears loved it. It was all part of the show.

Please don't judge. It was a different era. As soon as zoo dieticians and veterinarians realized that gelatinous sugary confections were not healthy options for giant carnivorous beasts, the practice was halted. Today, the Great Bear Wilderness exhibit at Brookfield Zoo features polar bears whose mostly meat diet is carefully monitored. It's not as much fun, but keeping the bears healthy is the better choice.

In 2004, the Association of Zoos and Aquariums instituted the Polar Bear Species Survival Plan to balance genetic, demographic, and husbandry concerns including maintaining closed populations,

---

16. Hanneke Brooymans, "Adventurer witnessed effects of climate change," *Calgary Herald*, October 10, 2009, 10, https://www.newspapers.com/article/calgary-herald-the-greatest-threat-to-o/42705319/.

which further protects the integrity of polar bears in captivity and in the wild.[17] Plus, zoos like Brookfield lead research efforts, fill in knowledge gaps, cosponsor environmental protection efforts, and serve as ambassadors for vulnerable species like polar bears.

Having seen these animals up close, I can't imagine a world without polar bears. Efforts to save polar bears and any other endangered species should be applauded. God certainly approves. After all, the very first chapter of the Bible tells us that humankind was given responsibility to look after all animals, whether in captivity or the wild. *"Then God said, 'Let us make human beings in our image, to be like us. They will reign over the fish in the sea, the birds in the sky, the livestock, all the wild animals on the earth, and the small animals that scurry along the ground'"* (Genesis 1:26 NLT).

THE REVELATION OF WILDLIFE

Safeguarding all animals—including polar bears—is a box worth checking for so many reasons.

ANIMALS CAN BE A SOURCE OF KNOWLEDGE

"But ask the animals, and they will teach you, or the birds in the sky, and they will tell you; or speak to the earth, and it will teach you, or let the fish in the sea inform you" (Job 12:7–8).

THE PRESENCE OF ANIMALS CONFIRMS GOD'S PROVISION

"Consider the ravens: They do not sow or reap, they have no storeroom or barn; yet God feeds them. And how much more valuable you are than birds!" (Luke 12:24).

ANIMALS HELP US INTERPRET SCRIPTURE

From ants to donkeys to leviathans, the Bible incorporates animals in scores of memorable lessons. In Mark 10:25, Jesus said,

---

17. Katie Morell, "Polar Bears and AZA: Polar Bear Research at AZA-Accredited Facilities Helps Wild Cousins," Association of Zoos & Aquariums, May 21, 2020, https://www.aza. org/connect-stories/stories/polar-bear-research.

"It is easier for a camel to go through the eye of a needle than for someone who is rich to enter the kingdom of God."

ANIMALS POINT TO THE GLORY OF GOD

"Let everything that has breath praise the Lord. Praise the Lord" (Psalm 150:6).

Theologians frequently point to the majesty of a starry night as proof of a Creator. Psalm 19:1 affirms, *"The heavens declare the glory of God; the skies proclaim the work of his hands."* But an even better case for God's unpredictable creativity might be the diversity of the animal kingdom: the stripes on a zebra, the structure of a beehive, the slithering of a cobra, the colors of a peacock, and the splash of a humpback whale.

Let's all agree we need to save the polar bears, black rhinos, monarch butterflies, pygmy three-toed sloth, and every vulnerable or endangered species so that future generations can fully appreciate the glory of our God.

PERFECT DESIGN, PERFECTLY BALANCED

On an even broader scale, making the world a better place requires us to be responsible caretakers of all creation—both of the creatures themselves and of the places they call home. God has intricately designed all parts of His creation to work together in a perfectly balanced ecosystem. Consider how animals and humans take in oxygen and expel carbon dioxide, for example, while trees and plants do the opposite. Or think about the variety of animals in the food chain that we all learned about back in grade school.

Achieving the Great Commission—making disciples of all nations—presupposes a planet that can first sustain healthy life. Clean water is essential to survival. Advancements in scientific research and medicine are fueled by biodiversity. And a sustainable worldwide economy needs the foundation of a healthy planet. When Christians demonstrate concern—and even accountability—for the natural world, it opens the door for the gospel to go forth.

☑ CHECKING THE BOX

The idea that Christians and environmentalists would ever disagree about the importance of caring for natural resources and the health of our planet should be preposterous. Agreeing on the worthy goal of protecting wildlife would seem to be an easy conversation starter that could ultimately lead to even more in-depth sharing and collaboration toward making the world a better place.

TO PONDER OR SHARE...

☐ 1. How does nature point to God?

☐ 2. Do you recall other animals referenced in the Bible? For example, hyrax, locust, grasshopper, behemoth, stork, wolf, lion, a talking donkey, a lost sheep, or the cattle on a thousand hills?

☐ 3. Setting politics aside, do you generally agree with those who are aggressively focused on being environmentally responsible?

☐ 4. Why are Christians sometimes accused of being environmentally negligent? How can we reverse that reputation?

☐ 5. Next time you take a kid (or a friend) to the zoo, how can you use that time to share the gospel?

7

ASSEMBLE AN ENTOURAGE

"If you want to go fast, go alone.
If you want to go far, go together."
—African proverb

In your quest to make the world a better place, you may be tempted to be a lone wolf, blaze your own trail, march to the beat of your own drum, and be the master of your own destiny.

The benefits of that approach are many. You set your own goals and make your own schedule. You don't have to deal with slackers or drag along any deadweight freeloaders. There's no one to throw cold water on your brilliant ideas. Best of all, when you check a box or two, you can take all the credit.

Sound good? Well, not so fast. Many platitudes in favor of teamwork suggest a different story. Two heads are better than one. Many hands make light work. There's strength in numbers. United we stand, divided we fall. The more, the merrier. Teamwork makes the dream work.

After considering both options, the question remains: *Should I strive to work alone or in collaboration with others?*

Here's the way to have the best of both worlds. First, hand-pick your posse. Surround yourself with people who have the same moral code, work ethic, and lofty goals, but who also have different skill sets from you. Second, block out some time every week to do your own thing. That might be researching, writing, personal brainstorming, or setting priorities in your life. Third, recognize that while every individual has value, there is only room in your posse for a select few. With gentleness and respect, be intentional about easing people in and out of your circle of influence.

Collaboration can be challenging. It requires vulnerability, being open to feedback, trust, compromise, and sometimes setting aside your own agenda for the welfare of the team. Plus, you may endure the aggravation of meaningless meetings! The Bible warns that working with others can sometimes lead to more talk than action. *"All hard work brings a profit, but mere talk leads only to poverty"* (Proverbs 14:23). In the end, surrounding yourself with a trustworthy network of friends and colleagues has great benefits.

A dependable team of friends and advisors—within a company, small group, family, or social network—gets high marks from the Bible. By definition, your posse improves the lives of others. Initially, the benefits extend to those in your inner circle, but then they spread to everyone whose lives they touch.

> *Two are better than one, because they have a good return for their labor: If either of them falls down, one can help the other up. But pity anyone who falls and has no one to help them up.* (Ecclesiastes 4:9–10)

> *Let us consider how we may spur one another on toward love and good deeds, not giving up meeting together, as some are in the habit of doing, but encouraging one another—and all the more as you see the Day approaching.* (Hebrews 10:24–25)

> *Encourage one another and build one another up, just as you also are doing.* (1 Thessalonians 5:11 NASB)

THE BENEFITS OF TEAMWORK

SMALL GROUPS ENCOURAGE NETWORKING

Because each member has different gifts and experiences, there's a chance that someone in your posse can provide expertise in just about anything that needs to get done, whether moving a refrigerator, creating a website, stuffing a turkey, or interpreting a challenging passage of Scripture.

PURPOSEFUL DEBATE CLARIFIES THE MISSION

Not only are two heads better than one—two heads are also better than two! Famously, the Wright brothers squabbled and debated over the design of the first airplane. In the process, they also mastered the art of critical thinking, often switching sides and debating in support of the opposing argument. Said Orville, "Often, after an hour or so of heated argument, we would discover that we were as far from agreement as when we started, but that each had changed to the other's original position."[18]

COLLABORATION MULTIPLIES EFFECTIVENESS

Extraordinary goals require extraordinary teamwork. While Robert Oppenheimer, the director of the Los Alamos Laboratory, was credited with developing the first atomic bomb that ultimately ushered in the end of World War II, the Manhattan Project employed at its peak 130,000 scientists, engineers, and military personnel in a coordinated effort to realize its goal.[19]

TRUSTWORTHY ADVISORS PROVIDE ACCOUNTABILITY

Lost in our own world, we may get tunnel vision and begin to think life is all about us. Proverbs 27:17 reminds us, "*As iron sharpens iron, so one person sharpens another.*" Entrusting your hopes, dreams, goals, and fears to others gives those people permission to challenge

18. Mickey Mellen, "Argue Like the Wright Brothers," Medium, February 19, 2021, https://mickmel.medium.com/argue-like-the-wright-brothers-b4948febbf7d.
19, "Manhattan Project Background Information and Preservation Work," Office of Legacy Management, US Department of Energy, https://www.energy.gov/lm/manhattan-project-background-information-and-preservation-work#:

your assumptions and, as necessary, steer you toward course corrections in your life journey. Your circle can help you get life right.

Being part of an intentional weekly small group keeps you from stagnating. More than likely, sometime during your regular gatherings, there's a time to "go around the table" and give an update on life in general. There shouldn't be any pressure to report any amazing or miraculous news. Just be authentic. Don't make stuff up. Knowing you'll be asked to share an update can spur you to step out and make a change or take a chance with that next project or outreach.

☑ CHECKING THE BOX

> In your quest to make the world a better place, start with your own small circle of friends and family. Then, with intentionality, broaden your sphere of influence. If everyone in your posse has that attitude, even better!

TO PONDER OR SHARE...

- ☐ 1. When are you a lone wolf? When do you rely on your wolf pack?

- ☐ 2. Are you part of a small group that meets regularly? If not, identify three or four people who would make awesome members and toss out the idea of meeting weekly.

- ☐ 3. If you are already in a small group, do you get deep, or is it mostly superficial chitchat?

- ☐ 4. Describe the perfect small group. How many people? Where and when to meet? What to cover? What to try to avoid?

- ☐ 5. Does your church encourage participation in small groups? If not, how can you spur your church body to get on board with Hebrews 10:24–25?

8

CREATE UPLIFTING ART

"An artist earns the right to call himself a creator only when he admits to himself that he is but an instrument."[20]
—Henry Miller

Somehow in the last generation or two, art and faith have gone their separate ways. Would you agree?

For hundreds of years, the greatest art in all the world was created to honor or point others to God. From a Christian perspective, that includes extraordinary paintings such as da Vinci's *The Last Supper*, Francesca's *The Resurrection*, and Raphael's *Sistine Madonna*. The Bible also inspired classical composers Bach, Handel, Haydn, Mendelssohn, to name a few. World-renowned architecture, exhibits, literature, and even epic films from before this century frequently explored and elevated biblical themes.

Indeed, all the world's leading religions at one time brought us breathtaking art including sculptures, temples, mosques, textiles, and jewelry. Even masks, headdresses, and totem poles honored unseen gods. Unfortunately, today's art seems motivated by lesser ideals. Class warfare. Consumerism. Personal agendas. Political turmoil. Even art created by AI without human oversight.

---

20. Henry Miller, *The Time of Assassins: A Study of Rimbaud* (New York: New Directions Publishing, 1946), 138.

It's not difficult to find "shock value" art that purports to "make a statement" but is really just an attention grab from an artist. Examples include Andres Serrano's *Immersion (Piss Christ)* (a photograph of a crucifix in a jar of urine), Tracey Emin's *My Bed* (an unmade bed surrounded by used condoms, underwear, and empty alcohol bottles), and the infamous exhibit *Vorm – Fellows – Attitude* in Rotterdam, The Netherlands, from the art collective Gelitin, featuring what can only be described as four giant sculptures of feces. (Really.)

Slasher movies, porn novels, and music lyrics that are blasphemous or demean women are all examples of creativity that's really not very creative. Artists—especially those who accept grants from the National Endowment for the Arts—have the responsibility to leave audiences glad they were witnesses to their art. If audience members feel like they need to take showers after attending an exhibit, watching a video, or hearing a song, the artist has failed.

For sure, art has the unique ability to provoke new ideas and encourage discourse. Not every painting has to be filled with daisies. Not every movie has to end with the hero and heroine riding off into the sunset. Choreography should sometimes leave the dancer off balance. A symphony should include minor chords. Artists should have the freedom to expose the dark side of our world, but is it too much to ask that today's artists also cultivate noble ideals and motivate their audiences to pursue virtuous, elegant, or heroic aspirations?

By the way, notoriety or popularity should not be the deciding factor of whether art is really art. Moths are drawn to flames. Motorists rubberneck to look at car wrecks. Just because critics swoon, a venue sells out, or a line snakes out the entrance, that doesn't mean an exhibition or performance has any redeeming value.

So how can art make the world a better place?

THE POTENTIAL POWER OF ART

ART FOSTERS COMMUNITY

Public art museums, festivals, and workshops encourage strangers to engage with each other while inviting collaboration and mutual art appreciation within communities.

ART BRIDGES THE LANGUAGE GAP

Many forms of the visual arts require no verbal communication. Art can celebrate cultural heritage and promote appreciation for all nationalities. The world becomes smaller.

MUSIC AND DANCE ARE PART OF A UNIVERSAL LANGUAGE

Melodies, rhythms, and dance transcend cultural, linguistic, and social barriers. Diversity in the world of music proves that every culture has the ability to elevate the human spirit.

ART SEPARATES US FROM THE ANIMALS

Humans are the only creatures who appreciate creativity. Do you think a shark appreciates the astonishing beauty of the fish swarming a coral reef? He's just grazing for dinner. Does a wildebeest appreciate the sunset on the African savannah? He's just biding his time as part of the food chain. The creative process celebrates humanity.

ART GIVES GLORY TO THE CREATOR

That's what God created us to do—give glory back to Him. So, make your artistry—in any form—an offering. Worship the Lord in splendor. "*Ascribe to the* Lord *the glory due his name; bring an offering and come before him. Worship the* Lord *in the splendor of his holiness*" (1 Chronicles 16:29).

The best way to respond to art that drags humanity down is to create and engage with art that uplifts. On your refrigerator, in your living room, in your community, and as you travel, do your part to curate, design, style, and invest in art with a mission. That's an easy and personally satisfying box to check.

For centuries the most brilliant musicians, artists, and writers lived with one purpose and passion—to honor God. You may not think of yourself as a Michelangelo, da Vinci, Handel, Bach, Bunyan, or Tolkien. But you'll never know how your work will impact others until you step out in faith. The art form doesn't matter. From dance to weaving to calligraphy, it could be anything.

☑ CHECKING THE BOX

> Where do you start? You already know. Follow the clear instructions of Philippians 4:8: *"Finally, brothers and sisters, whatever is true, whatever is noble, whatever is right, whatever is pure, whatever is lovely, whatever is admirable—if anything is excellent or praiseworthy—think about such things."*

TO PONDER OR SHARE...

☐ 1. When was the last time you were moved or deeply impacted by a piece of art, film, song, book, or performance? Did it somehow point to God?

☐ 2. Who's your favorite artist, no matter the medium? What do they mean to you?

☐ 3. Why might someone support art that offends?

☐ 4. Is it possible that creating and appreciating art is one of the characteristics that separates humans from animals?

☐ 5. Beyond art, what is Philippians 4:8 referencing?

9

OPEN YOUR ARMS

"When we forgive, we set a prisoner free and then discover
that the prisoner we set free was us."[21]
—Lewis B. Smedes

Not sure why, but most of the people in your circle of influence find it hard to apologize. Right? Even if they regret having messed up, they can never seem to find the right opportunity or the right words to express sincere remorse and get a broken relationship back on track.

Why might that be? It could be that pride gets in the way. Some may think admitting they were wrong makes them appear weak. Maybe they're afraid of becoming a scapegoat for future mishaps. Once you admit guilt, that label is hard to shake. From a legal perspective, admitting fault can result in repercussions that cost you time, money, and freedom.

Reconciliation might be impossible because the injured party has closed the door to communication. That's unfortunate. When a sincere apology meets a brick wall, the rift deepens. Both parties tend to dig in their heels, and the relationship is likely to crumble.

Holding a grudge or carrying a chip on your shoulder is an ongoing theme addressed in the Bible. Examples include Pharaoh's

21. Lewis B. Smedes, *Forgive and Forget: Healing the Hurts We Don't Deserve*, reprinted with Foreword ([New York?]: HarperCollins, 1984; San Francisco: HarperCollins, 1996), x.

hardened heart, which led to the devastating series of plagues on Egypt (see Exodus 7:13–12:32). In the wilderness, the Israelites turned callous against God even while their needs were being met miraculously by provisions of manna, quail, and water (see Exodus 16). In Mark 10:17–22, Jesus's candid instruction to *"sell everything you have and give to the poor"* (verse 21) hardened the heart of the rich young ruler. Certainly, the Pharisees, Judas, and the soldiers who mocked Jesus on the cross experienced hearts turned to stone.

Fortunately, Jesus gave us a vivid example of a loving heart that was not hardened. Most readers of the parable of the prodigal son (see Luke 15:11–32) focus on the lesson for anyone who is lost, hungry, and seeking redemption: you can and should go home to the father. Well, that's only part of the story. The actions of the father in the parable model the *other* side of how to respond during interpersonal conflict.

As you can imagine, the father was regularly scanning the horizon, praying for the safe return of his rebellious son. There was no malice in that father's heart. Only love. But the son didn't know that. He imagined returning home would mean being treated like one of his father's servants. The prodigal young man even decided he would be okay with that arrangement.

So, he got up and went to his father.

> But while he was still a long way off, his father saw him and was filled with compassion for him; he ran to his son, threw his arms around him, and kissed him. The son said to him, "Father, I have sinned against heaven and against you. I am no longer worthy to be called your son." But the father said to his servants, "Quick! Bring the best robe and put it on him. Put a ring on his finger and sandals on his feet. Bring the fattened calf and kill it. Let's have a feast and celebrate. For this son of mine was dead and is alive again; he was lost and is found." So they began to celebrate.   (Luke 15:20–24)

This reception should serve as a model for anyone who has been wronged. When someone comes to you with sincere regrets, your best response is to run to them with open arms. A strong-willed son, a wayward sibling, a onetime friend, maybe even a stranger or enemy—if it's at all possible, eagerly accept their apology. Make no demands or conditions. Maybe even throw a little bit of a party.

It's easy to build walls. To hold a grudge. Especially when someone has done you wrong. One school of psychology vehemently recommends cutting anyone who mistreats you out of your life. In some cases, that's the right thing to do. But what if we kept the door open—and our arms open—eager to forgive? Might that be a better box to check?

THE BENEFITS OF FORGIVING

FORGIVENESS OPENS THE DOOR TO COMMUNICATION

We all mess up. But we will never learn from those mistakes if we stay inside our own heads. When you humble yourself enough to admit you were wrong or extend a hand of forgiveness, the conflict can be instantly resolved. In the end, both parties actually become stronger, wiser, and even closer.

HOLDING A GRUDGE MEANS YOU LOSE

Those with a hardened heart add to their own suffering. Long after the original wrongdoing is forgotten, holding on to resentment distracts you from any purpose, fulfillment, and satisfaction life has for you. Grudges are joy killers and life-sucking burdens. It's difficult to smile when excess bile is eating away at your stomach lining. According to the Mayo Clinic, letting go of a grudge can even lower blood pressure, ease depression, and strengthen your immune system.[22] Reduced bitterness makes the world a better place.

---

22. Mayo Clinic Staff, "Forgiveness: Letting Go of Grudges and Bitterness," Healthy Lifestyle Adult Health, Mayo Clinic, https://www.mayoclinic.org/healthy-lifestyle/adult-health/in-depth/forgiveness/art-20047692.

FOLDING YOUR ARMS KEEPS FRIENDS AWAY

Sending out a vibe signaling indignation or contempt doesn't keep just one enemy at bay. It shuts you off to potential partners, colleagues, old friends, and new loves.

CELEBRATING RESTORED RELATIONSHIPS HEALS COMMUNITIES

Social media means that, more than ever, the world is watching. Any rift you perpetuate may be cheered or sneered. But social media also facilitates the rapid spread of news regarding restoration. And just maybe when you roast the fatted calf, others will join the feast.

CREATE A SAFE SPACE FOR ADDITIONAL CONVERSATIONS

The parable of the prodigal son concludes with what might be the most powerful conversation of all. (See Luke 15:25–32.) Sparked by the events of the day, the father has a touching heart-to-heart with his hardworking and envious older son. That new understanding between the generations never would have happened without the father's open arms for the younger brother.

If you haven't done so for a while, go ahead and open your Bible to the parable of the prodigal son. Read it three times in order to consider the events from the perspective of the three main characters. Identify ways in which the father's actions—running to his lost son—made the *entire region* a better place. The older brother was reassured of his father's devotion. The wealthy family was reunited. Word spread among the attendees at that evening's celebration. The good news may even have reached the pig farmer and the prodigal son's former party crew in that distant country.

☑ CHECKING THE BOX

Reconciliation ripples outward, bringing positive impact that extends way beyond the original parties in any dispute. When grudge-filled division seems inevitable or unending, restoration may still be possible. However, it will take two courageous decisions: one by the individual who decides—in humility and without any guarantees—to offer some kind of olive branch or white flag, and the other by the individual who chooses to watch the horizon and run with open arms at the first sign of that peace offering.

TO PONDER OR SHARE...

- ☐ 1. What grudges or unforgiveness are you holding? From whom should you be seeking forgiveness?

- ☐ 2. Beyond the two parties involved, can you see how the healing of a rift can actually impact many other people—especially family members and concerned friends?

- ☐ 3. Is there value in forgiving someone for a wrongdoing if they are not repentant?

- ☐ 4. With which of the three main characters in the parable of the prodigal son do you most identify? (Or are you more like the partygoers or the pigs?)

- ☐ 5. Like the father in the parable, are you waiting for someone to come home? What if you went out looking for them?

10

RECOGNIZE YOU HAVE
A PURPOSE

"The place God calls you to is the place where your deep
gladness and the world's deep hunger meet."[23]
—Frederick Buechner

When you were little, did you ever have a well-meaning, slightly creepy aunt or uncle ask you what you wanted to be when you grew up? To humor them, you gave some corny answer and, in reply, they gave an odd chuckle and patted you on the head.

At the time, you didn't dare share your biggest dreams or darkest fears. Your honest words would have left them startled and unhinged. Still, their question got you thinking and wondering, "What is my purpose? Why am I here? Can I give voice to my dreams?"

All excellent questions.

A few years later, another well-meaning adult—a parent, teacher, youth pastor, or grandparent—may have said, "You can be anything you want to be!" Well, that kind of statement can give you hope, but it also puts on a lot of pressure. Suddenly you've added another item on your already lengthy must-do list.

---

23. Frederick Buechner, *Wishful Thinking* ([San Francisco?]: Harper One, 1993). Accessed via Frederick Buechner Center website, https://www.frederickbuechner.com/quote-of-the-day/2017/7/18/vocation (accessed March 10, 2024).

Somehow you are expected to meet the perfect soulmate, make lifelong friends, connect with God, make your bed every morning, wear clean underwear in case you get in a car accident, *and* find a promising career.

A few more years later—after contemplating all you have to do—another series of questions pops into your head. "What if none of this matters? Is it possible that this is all there is? What if every person on the planet is just a worthless ghost walking around in a meat-covered skeleton? Is it possible that work, hobbies, friends, enemies, lovers, and pretty much everything we think is important is ultimately meaningless?"

Well, yes and no. Stay with me here.

This earth is temporary. In the grand scheme, those things that seem so important—your stock portfolio, having perfect teeth, bowling a three hundred game, knowing all the words to "American Pie," and your world record in stacking Oreos—really don't matter. Certainly, all our possessions for which we worked so hard will one day be gone. The truth remains: You can't take it with you. After all, you've never seen a hearse pulling a U-Haul trailer.

Even Solomon—the wisest person aside from Jesus who ever lived—wrote, *"Utterly meaningless! Everything is meaningless"* (Ecclesiastes 1:2). But please don't take that literally. Solomon had looked around and concluded rightfully that any and all *earthly* pursuits and passions have no long-term value. In contrast, Solomon would be the first to confirm that, if it relates to God and eternity, we're talking about *infinite* value.

To be clear, the idea of your "purpose" goes far beyond your moneymaking career. Any activity you perform—growing crops, building skyscrapers, loading the dishwasher, taking out the trash, rocking newborns, playing the fiddle, running for mayor, writing a term paper, delivering a sermon, assembling widgets, or healing the sick—can be a noble pursuit. But only if you are simultaneously pursuing God's will for your life. Which, by the way, He has planned especially for you.

Ephesians 2:10 confirms, *"For we are God's handiwork, created in Christ Jesus to do good works, which God prepared in advance for us to do."*

So, how does it feel to realize there already exists a rock-solid meaningful plan for your life? That you have worthwhile work to do? You are not an accident. You have a purpose. And, what's more, that plan was inaugurated before time began.

It's possible that reading these words in this chapter in this book constitutes the first time you've been told you have a God-ordained purpose. It's exciting, isn't it? Other ways to describe it might be scary, exhilarating, puzzling, and humbling—to think that the Creator of the universe cares about who you are and what you will achieve with your life is truly mind-boggling.

PURSUING YOUR PURPOSE

As it turns out, everyone on the planet has their own set of boxes to check. They just haven't realized it. In God's design, every time an individual gains that personal revelation, the world becomes a better place.

KNOWING YOU HAVE PURPOSE LAUNCHES A GRATIFYING QUEST

Rather than just watching movies with heroes doing heroic things, your own life becomes an epic adventure. Anticipating future challenges inspires innovation and ultimately helps you reach your full potential. The pursuit of knowledge reveals clues you can apply to every facet of life. Cliffhangers awaken your capacity to defy the odds and conquer risk. Failures become opportunities to overcome obstacles and build resilience.

PURSUING HIGHER ASPIRATIONS REVEALS YOUR OWN LIMITS

Even as you sharpen your gifts, you will learn an inevitable lesson: You can't do it all. Your own success requires help, guidance, and teamwork. That's how your quest for purpose leads to community and partnership. When that happens, all those people in your growing circle of friends and colleagues begin to uncover their own capabilities and value.

BECOMING YOUR BEST SELF ELEVATES OTHERS

Whether they are watching you or partnering with you, others will be inspired to pursue their own God-given purpose by your quest for your purpose. It might be your example, your encouragement, or even a healthy competition that motivates your friends, coworkers, or even business competitors.

ETERNITY WILL REVEAL HOW GOD USES US TODAY

We won't fully know how we impact the world while we're in it. First Corinthians 13:12 (NLT) explains, *"Now we see things imperfectly, like puzzling reflections in a mirror, but then we will see everything with perfect clarity. All that I know now is partial and incomplete, but then I will know everything completely, just as God now knows me completely."*

As we create, speak, build, manage, teach, refine, grow, heal, write, deliver, or pursue any worthwhile task, we can trust that God has a plan for us to impact the lives of others. But don't even think about hogging that glory; our most impressive achievements are possible only with God's guiding hand.

Honestly, you may never be 100 percent sure of your exact day-to-day purpose in life. While God doesn't change, the world around you will be ever evolving. You will change, as well—growing and learning. A season of evaluating your gifts and calling will precede a fresh wave of confidence. A season of doubt will precede a leap of faith.

☑ CHECKING THE BOX

Never allow the distractions of the world to deflect you from your pursuit of God's purpose for your life—that is, to get to heaven and take as many people with you as possible.

TO PONDER OR SHARE...

☐ 1. When you were young, what did you want to be when you grew up?

☐ 2. Does the idea that God has prepared work for you leave you eager or befuddled?

☐ 3. What personal dreams of yours remain unspoken and unfulfilled?

☐ 4. Have you ever been stuck in the rut thinking your purpose in life was only related to your job and finances? What might be other reasons you exist?

☐ 5. What boxes have you checked in your life that now seem either irrelevant or a complete waste of time and energy? (Or might they be stepping stones to some future victory?)

11

HONOR YOUR PARENTS

"He that raises a large family, does indeed, while he lives to observe them, stand…a broader mark for sorrow; but then he stands a broader mark for pleasure too."[24]
—Benjamin Franklin

You have to love the fifth commandment. It's the only commandment that comes with a direct benefit. I may be overstating the promise, but Exodus 20:12 might be paraphrased, "Be nice to your parents, and you'll get a long life and real estate."

Read it for yourself: *"Honor your father and your mother, so that you may live long in the land the LORD your God is giving you."*

The idea of honoring your parents is not very popular these days. Young adults are blaming their moms and dads for their lack of confidence, poor people skills, inability to hold a job, the broken planet, gender confusion, and even their ability to work. In some cases, the younger generation may have a legitimate point. I recently heard a boomer father whining that his adult children didn't have any motivation to strive for excellence because they had grown up in bedrooms filled with participation trophies. I didn't have the heart to point out it was his generation that handed out all those trophies. So, who's really to blame?

24. Benjamin Franklin, *Memoirs of the Life and Writings of Benjamin Franklin, Vol. II* (London: 1818), 89, https://ia601601.us.archive.org/14/items/templefranklin02franrich/templefranklin02franrich.pdf.

Honoring your parents does not have to be a burden. If you're still living under their roof, it's actually pretty easy. Respect the house rules, pitch in on chores, show appreciation, and let them know where you're going and when you're coming home. As a father of five, I could come up with a hundred more rules, but you get the idea. Oh, yeah, it helps to throw your parents a bone once in a while. That means joining them at the kitchen table and sharing a recent life story. Something fun or surprising. Maybe offer them a peek at your hopes and dreams. Make them laugh. Make them glad they procreated.

If you're out of the house living on your own or married, parents still want to be a part of your life. Both generations can help build those bridges. Even in the best families, past verbal exchanges and harsh actions left from the years of raising or being a teenager can bleed into the present and cause residual remorse.

Now that you're all adults, somehow find a way to put those regrets behind you. Consider checking these boxes: make a sincere apology; acknowledge the challenges of that season of life; laugh at the folly of youth; marvel at the differing eras in which you grew up; or confess how much you cherish your relationship today. The goal is to transition those adversarial relationships into a mostly congenial and comfortable adult friendship.

The above strategies come in handy at any age. This week, you can get a smile from your own parents by shaking your head and sincerely asking, "How did you ever survive this season I'm experiencing right now?" Who knows? You may even get some solid advice.

Turning the tables, if you're a parent yearning to be honored by your adult children, there are things you can do. First, show them respect. Second, give words of affirmation. Every child at any age still wants to hear the words, "I am so proud of you." Third, keep storing up life lessons, but don't share unsolicited advice on parenting, careers, finances, or even spiritual matters. When they do come to you for wisdom, be gentle even as you expound on all the experience you've endured from the many mistakes you've made.

You may want to quote Proverbs 23:22, *"Listen to your father, who gave you life, and do not despise your mother when she is old."* But you may want to first take this advice from Titus 2:2-3, *"Teach the older men to be temperate, worthy of respect, self-controlled, and sound in faith, in love and in endurance. Likewise, teach the older women to be reverent in the way they live, not to be slanderers or addicted to much wine, but to teach what is good."*

NURTURING THE PARENT-CHILD RELATIONSHIP

Generational bonds within a family establish a foundation of confidence and courage to pursue goals that matter, make the family proud, and make the world a better place.

HONORING PARENTS FOSTERS A SENSE OF MUTUAL RESPECT

Adult children who stay in contact with their parents are often amazed at how mom and dad continue to be a valuable resource for life skills and perspectives that can't be found on any internet search.

TRADITIONS AND CULTURAL HERITAGE WON'T FADE

Older generations connect younger family members to the past. Recognizing and surrendering to family traditions creates an appreciation for diversity, awareness of changes in technology and culture, and promotes cross-generational interactions.

INTERGENERATIONAL INTERDEPENDENCE

Parents, grandparents, and great-grandparents invest much of their lives into future generations. That's no small thing and needs to be respectfully acknowledged. Later, those seniors may need the appreciative recipients of their years of love and generosity to reciprocate with financial resources, availability, proximity, compassion, common sense, and the wherewithal to communicate effectively with doctors, nurses, insurance providers, and senior living administrators. That's a key takeaway from the fifth commandment.

HONORING PARENTS SETS AN EXAMPLE FOR YOUR OWN CHILDREN

This may be a selfish motive, but never forget that children observe whether or not mom and dad honor grandma and grandpa. Your kids will likely be making critical life decisions for you in your old age. Families that care for each other ease the burden on society. Who cares most for seniors? Shouldn't it be their own children and grandchildren?

Finally, any discussion on honoring your parents may prompt the question with today's younger parents, *Should I have another kid?* The answer shouldn't be taken lightly. But if your current home is generally happy, healthy, and filled with love, another child or two will not just add to that love, they will *multiply* it. Plus, as the years unfold, having more kids increases your own opportunity to receive honor as a parent!

☑ CHECKING THE BOX

> Even though mistakes are made, parents should be honored. Honoring parents elevates a family and even promotes the value of making sure family members stay in touch, look out for each other, and care for Mom and Dad in their later years.

TO PONDER OR SHARE...

☐ 1. What are some fond memories from your childhood? Recall annual traditions or single events.

☐ 2. What are some traits or habits of your parents that are worth passing on to future generations? Which ones should not be passed on? And how will you break that chain?

☐ 3. Did reading this chapter stir negative memories? If so, what are some ways you can still honor the role of parents while beginning a healing process for multiple members of your extended family?

☐ 4. If you have siblings, what role will each of you play in honoring your parents?

☐ 5. Looking back as an adult, can you better understand some of the choices made by your parents?

12

CHAT WITH STRANGERS

"Strangers are friends that we some day may meet."[25]
—Edgar Guest

Not sure who or what is to blame, but the idea of striking up a conversation with a perfect stranger is inconceivable to most people these days. Why might that be?

Are we all just too busy and can't be bothered? Have we become so overloaded by our own routines and responsibilities that there's no time for spontaneous social interactions? That would be a shame.

Maybe we're scared or anxious. Growing up, the idea of "stranger danger" was pounded into our heads, which left us fearful of anyone we didn't know. Plus, a generation ago we typically surrounded ourselves with people from the same cultural background with the same worldview. Today, we've come to appreciate the value of diversity, but still, we hesitate because we don't want inadvertently to offend someone from a different background.

Earbuds might be the culprit. Before the tech boom, it was acceptable—or even expected—to break the uncomfortable silence when you found yourself sharing a park bench, sitting next to a stranger on a plane, or standing in a long line with someone you'd never met. Now, almost no one is sitting or standing in silence;

25. Edgar A. Guest, poem, "Faith," *The Boston Globe*, August 19, 1915, 10, column 4 (reprinted from *The Detroit Free Press*).

they're too busy listening to their favorite podcast or musician, so we dare not interrupt by striking up a conversation.

There's also the possibility that engaging a stranger could end badly. You politely say "hi," and they shout obscenities or look at you in disgust. That may be an unlikely response out in public, but online, it's almost routine. Perhaps we too often blame social media for what's wrong with the world, but there's validity to that concern. Why take a chance at exposing ourselves to meanness or ridicule?

Turning the corner, let's consider the benefits of engaging in this risky behavior—of choosing to strike up a conversation with a perfect stranger.

Check that box and you might learn something, such as when the next train is due, where to go for sushi, how to play hopscotch, or what's going on with the crowd of people down the block. You might make a friend. You might make a routine flight memorable. You might become a better listener and communicator. By opening up to a stranger, you might even gain an unconventional resolution to a nagging personal problem that you could never have revealed to a friend or relative.

BENEFITS OF COMMUNICATING WITH STRANGERS

More than that, talking to strangers can make the world a better place. Not just for you, but for the people you meet, the people they meet, and so on.

ENGAGING WITH STRANGERS CREATES COMMUNITY

Even someone who prefers solitude craves a sense of belonging and has needs they can't meet on their own. A kind word to an introvert establishes trust and interdependence. The goal is not to force them out of their comfort zone but rather to let them know that, when they are ready to talk or if they ever need something, they are not alone and have somewhere to turn.

NEW ACQUAINTANCES FOSTER NEW FRIENDSHIPS

Every friend you will ever have was once a stranger. You may only have a handful of true-blue friends in your life. But no matter what, there is certainly room for one more person who needs a friend and can be a friend.

STRANGERS NEED TO KNOW THE THINGS YOU KNOW

If you keep it to yourself, all that wisdom and experience you've gained over the years will fail to realize its full potential. Remember the unexpected solution you discovered to that dilemma you faced years ago? Someone in your community is struggling with that same issue this very day. You could be the stranger who comes to their rescue with wisdom or a helping hand.

STRANGERS BY DEFINITION HAVE DIFFERENT BACKGROUNDS

Collaborating with likeminded colleagues with the same experience tends to get the same results. Synergy and breakthrough ideas increase when contradictory or divergent characters put their heads together. Strangers may disagree or attack the same problem from different angles, but those opposing viewpoints open the door to new and infinite possibilities.

STRANGERS NEED LOVE TOO

The command to love your neighbor extends down the street, across the countryside, and to the ends of the earth. Jesus's instruction in Mark 16:15 to *"go into all the world and preach the gospel to all creation"* is the most profound way to love, and it describes the most important chat any stranger will ever have.

☑ CHECKING THE BOX

It may be reasonable not to trust strangers. But it's worth remembering that, to strangers, you're a stranger too. With the next stranger you meet, consider them a fellow explorer on this adventure called life. Be safe. Be smart.

But it's probable you might learn something from them that God can use in your own life today or down the road. By the way, that stranger may have much more to offer than you could imagine. Hebrews 13:2 suggests one surprising reason to roll out the red carpet: *"Do not forget to show hospitality to strangers, for by so doing some people have shown hospitality to angels without knowing it."*

TO PONDER OR SHARE...

☐ 1. Are you afraid of strangers? Did you ever consider that you're a stranger to others?

☐ 2. What if you smiled more? First, check your smile in the mirror. Is it creepy or welcoming? (Hint: Smile with your eyes!)

☐ 3. Are there places where it's easier to talk to strangers?

☐ 4. Is your church welcoming to strangers?

☐ 5. How did you meet your best friend(s)?

13

DON'T JUST PROMISE TO PRAY

"True prayer is measured by weight, and not by length. A single groan before God may have more fullness of prayer in it than a fine oration of great length."[26]
—Charles Spurgeon

I don't like to break promises, so I try not to make too many of them. That's also why, when I'm in a group setting and someone shares a sincere prayer request, I am not the first to chirp, "I'll pray for you."

To be clear, I believe prayer works. Prayer is critical to knowing God's will and living your best life. When a friend asks for prayer, I truly believe any humble prayer I make will be heard and answered by a loving God. Still, I know I often get caught up in my own personal (and less important) pursuits and fail to follow through on my promise.

Is there a way to counteract this undeniable problem? Let's kick it around.

First, let's all agree that the current word choice by members of the media is both accurate and unfortunate. Sometime in the last decade or so, newscasters stopped saying, "Our thoughts and prayers are with you." In years past, after hearing of some tragedy

---

26. Charles Spurgeon, "The Secret of Power in Prayer," *Metropolitan Tabernacle Pulpit* Vol. 34 Sermon 2002, 1888.

or difficulty, an interviewer would say those gentle words as a way of expressing a caring attitude and inviting the greater community to literally follow up with prayer. In today's post-Christian culture, the phrase has been shortened to, "Our thoughts are with you." In many ways, that's understandable. It would be hypocritical to promise prayers that will never happen. Plus, we certainly can't mention prayer in public because that would upset atheists.

The second part of this discussion regards how we, as Christians, can improve our follow-through on promises to pray. The truth is, most of us are forgetful and probably need to devise a method for recording and tracking prayer requests—lest we forget what we've promised to pray for. You could do it the old-fashioned way with a pen and journal, but I recommend making positive use of the technology that often gets blamed for undermining Christian values. Next time someone asks for your prayers, pull out your smartphone—right then and there—and use a prayer app to help you track your prayers and remind you to pray. Apps like PrayerMate, Echo Prayer, Ora, Christian Prayer Prompter, Prayer Notebook, or OnlinePrayerJournal. As you can imagine, these apps include a variety of links and ways to connect, track, and forward prayers requests.

One possible strategy for keeping your promise to pray would be to spend intentional time at the end of every day recalling all your interactions. Since waking up this morning, did you wave at your neighbor, tickle your toddler, talk to Mom on the phone, text your BFF, yell at an umpire, curse the driver in the giant SUV, walk quickly past the panhandler, kiss your spouse, scream at your teenager, read a news alert about the president, talk with old work colleague, or sneer at a barista who was having his own bad day? All of those individuals need your prayer.

In one sense, all you have to do is say, "Heavenly Father— everyone I met today—please draw each one of them close to you. Amen." God knows their exact needs, and He will honor your prayers. But there's something satisfying about submitting our specific, thoughtful requests to an all-powerful, all-knowing God. He wants us to dig deep into our own heart and be fully aware of the needs of others. Prayers need to be grounded in devotion and sincerity. The Bible confirms, "*The effective, fervent prayer of a righteous man avails much*" (James 5:16 NKJV).

All of the above are valid strategies, but this one might be even better: Pray right then and there. When someone shares a prayer request—big or small—ask if you can pray right on the spot. Or just launch into a short prayer without asking permission. "Heavenly Father, we know you love us and care about every aspect of our lives. Right now...."

Your friend who asked for prayer will be caught off guard and delighted. Taking this one step further, try that same praying-in-the-moment strategy with someone who is sharing a concern but has *not* asked for prayer. Maybe they don't even believe in God.

I am not a heroic prayer warrior, but twice in recent months, neighbors in my cul-de-sac have expressed concerns about dramatic needs. A kidney transplant and a prodigal son. Moved by the Spirit, in both cases, I said, "Can we pray about that?" Both times, my neighbors were grateful for the short and politely assertive prayer. And both times, God's answer was affirmative and swift. A kidney was found and continues to do what kidneys do. And the young man reunited with his family.

PRAYER IN THE HERE AND NOW

Allow me to reaffirm, if you promise to keep your promise, then go ahead and promise to pray. But please consider checking the box that turns you into a person that prays right out loud in the moment—simply, sincerely, and expectantly—always remembering that you may not be able to change the world, but God can.

PRAYING IN THE MOMENT CAN BE INSTRUCTIVE

Many people think they have to kneel, fold their hands, be in church, or clean up their act before they can start to pray. Your proactive in-the-moment prayer may be wonderfully radical to some people. And when they see how your prayer is answered, even more so!

YOU DON'T HAVE TO CEASE ALL ACTIVITY TO PRAY

Prayer should be an ongoing component of every moment of the day. That idea is confirmed in the seemingly impossible command in 1 Thessalonians 5:17 to *"pray without ceasing"* (NASB). But really, it is quite doable because we're in constant connection with God through the indwelling of the Holy Spirit.

PROMISING TO PRAY PROVIDES HOPE

As you finish any conversation that has touched on personal needs, brokenness, fears, or aspirations, it is certainly a heartening gesture to promise continued prayer for days to come. That helps all involved know that the story is not over. Faith and hope endure. God has *"plans to prosper you and not to harm you, plans to give you hope and a future"* (Jeremiah 29:11).

YOUR PROMISE TO PRAY HOLDS YOU ACCOUNTABLE

Do your neighbors and coworkers even know that you're a follower of Christ? That you attend church? That you believe in prayer? When you pray aloud to God with sincere words from your own heart, you're finally admitting your identity in Christ to those within earshot. Of course, that means your life is now a showcase for that identity.

I hope you have a prayer closet where you can do battle with Satan. But sometimes you need to take that battle to the street. Out in public. The world needs to see how God works. How prayer works.

☑ CHECKING THE BOX

In the next few days, you will encounter a situation that could use some serious intervention from the Creator of the universe. A sick kid. A rough patch in a marriage. A family member going through a crisis. A wayward teen. A personal spiritual desert. Because you believe in the power of prayer, go ahead and use your human determination to say, "I'll pray for you." Then take the next step of following the guidance of the Holy Spirit *and pray.*

TO PONDER OR SHARE...

☐ 1. Have you ever said, "I'll pray for you" and then forgotten to follow through? (Worse, have you ever said "I'll pray for you" simply because you wanted to end a tedious conversation?)

☐ 2. Would you have any trouble praying out loud for someone who shared a desperate situation?

☐ 3. Do you believe prayer works? Have you experienced answered prayer in your own life?

☐ 4. Have you ever considered the possibility (or impossibility) of 1 Thessalonians 5:17 which instructs us to *"pray without ceasing"* (NASB)?

☐ 5. In general, should we pray longer, shorter, more frequently, more openly, or more expectantly? Should you change how you pray?

14

DO WHAT'S RIGHT IN FRONT OF YOU

"Just do it."
—Trademarked slogan, *Nike*, 1988

For some readers, this might be a stunning thought: *To make the world a better place you don't have to reinvent yourself.*[27]

Maybe you don't have to check any of these boxes that are often recommended by experts and non-experts alike: Quit your job. Take a battery of fill-in-the-blank personality tests. Travel to some distant mountain in search of the meaning of life. Sit across from a life coach through twenty very expensive sessions during which you are grilled about your childhood, career choices, passions, frustrations, hopes, and dreams.

There exists a much simpler method for launching your personal quest for global betterment. *Do what's right in front of you.*

Too many people spend their lives waiting for a sign. Others wait for a boss, coach, pastor, BFF, parent, book, blog, or magazine article to tell them what to do and how much energy to put into it. But if we just open our eyes, opportunities to make the world a better place are within our reach this very day.

---

27. This chapter adapted in part from Jay Payleitner, What If God Wrote Your Bucket List? (Eugene, OR: Harvest House Publishers, 2015), pp. 110-111.

The Bible puts it this way, "*Whatever your hand finds to do, do it with all your might*" (Ecclesiastes 9:10). Sound too easy? Maybe it is, maybe it isn't. But it's the right place to start. The challenge is to see the world—especially what's right in front of you—through God's eyes. For sure, you want to develop big picture thinking and vision that sees into eternity. But that begins by seeing the projects and possibilities right at your fingertips.

Recognize that God has your best interest in mind. Proverbs 3:6 (NLT) confirms, "*Seek his will in all you do, and he will show you which path to take.*" When a pathway opens, just take it. Put one foot in front of the other. Walk with conviction and determination. At this moment in time, your next box to check might be wonderfully clear.

Are there dirty dishes in the sink? Does the school board need someone with a Christian worldview? Does your elderly neighbor's porch need a coat of paint? Is your daughter, niece, or little sister preparing a tea party?

Your assignment is clear. Do the dishes. Run for school board. Paint the porch. Sit on a tiny chair and sip pretend tea.

And make sure you do it with all your might. Scrub that casserole dish until it gleams. Run your campaign with integrity and stand firm on issues of morality and religious freedom. Whistle while you paint. And extend your pinky properly as you sip your tea and perhaps even utilize your finest British accent as you chit-chat with the young hostess.

What task has God placed right in front of you? Sure, there may be someone else who could do it better or faster. You could ask the government for help. You could write long-winded editorials about what needs to be done. But there's something noble, instructional, mind-expanding, and liberating about the act of doing it yourself.

What are you doing with your summer? Or your weekend? Or the next ten minutes? If and when you find something that needs doing, do it with all your heart, mind, and strength. Even before that task is complete, you will have made the world a better place.

KEYS TO GETTING STARTED

DO YOUR PART

If everyone did what was right in front of them, everything would get done.

LET OTHERS DO THEIR PART

When we take over someone else's job, several possibly undesirable things happen. That person doesn't get the experience or satisfaction of completing a task. They may also feel belittled or marginalized. The task might be completed incorrectly. And your own assignments remain incomplete.

YOU DON'T HAVE TO DO IT ALL

Often just getting started on the task at hand motivates someone else to come alongside and partner in your project. That allows each participant to check their own box, cooperating for the greater good.

TRUST THE END GAME

Envisioning the final product and laying the groundwork is never a waste. The Bible teaches, *"Suppose one of you wants to build a tower. Won't you first sit down and estimate the cost to see if you have enough money to complete it?"* (Luke 14:28). At the same time, don't let the planning prevent you from doing it. Trust that the final execution is under God's control. *"Commit to the Lord whatever you do, and he will establish your plans"* (Proverbs 16:3).

Your calling may eventually take you to the other side of the planet, but don't book your flight quite yet. Within minutes of your home, there's work to be done. Of course, it might be backbreaking, mind-boggling, or soul-expanding work that requires you to step outside your comfort zone. But worry not, you have everything you need.

Consider: A day volunteering in a food kitchen. An overnight visiting the urban homeless. An afternoon doing prison visitations. A Sunday morning volunteering in the children's ministry at your home church. A week babysitting your neighbor's toddler while she's in the hospital. Dropping a sizable anonymous gift in the Salvation Army kettle. Providing sidewalk counseling outside a Planned Parenthood clinic. Delivering an Angel Tree gift to the children of an inmate. Or any other opportunity God puts on your heart. Any or all of the above can be world changing.

☑ CHECKING THE BOX

Don't compare your calling with others. There are too many unknowns. Your perception may be that someone is sacrificing way more than you. Or that someone else is a sluggard compared to your generosity and hard work. Don't go there. Focus on what God has called you to do. That's why "doing what's right in front of you" is such a compelling and rewarding challenge. That task is yours. And yours alone.

TO PONDER OR SHARE...

☐ 1. What task that needs doing is literally right in front of you?

☐ 2. What task that needs doing have you been putting off for day, months, or years?

☐ 3. Is your next obvious task not a project, but a person?

☐ 4. Are you a planner or a doer? Do you procrastinate or act impulsively?

☐ 5. Do you want to reinvent yourself? Or just be a better version of you?

15

EARN THE RIGHT TO OFFER YOUR OPINION

"The right to be heard does not automatically include the right to be taken seriously."[28]
—Hubert H. Humphrey

Just because you have an advanced degree, a high IQ, decades of experience, and a library of books you've actually read doesn't automatically give you permission to correct someone who is doing something different from the way you would do it.

Of course, there's a good chance you might be right. Your brilliant strategy could be just what the doctor ordered. You might have the exact right solution to a problem that is exasperating the entire class, congregation, company, country, or continent. But you still have to earn the right to be heard.

That's the way the world works. Your input may not be valued unless you've done your due diligence. And that's no small thing.

There are exceptions. Occasionally some fresh-faced teenager might be recruited as a virtuous voice from the wilderness. That hero-of-the moment, usually a girl not yet caught up in the cynical nature of our current world, is portrayed as a symbol of

28. Hubert Humphrey, "Address by Vice President Hubert Humphrey," (speech, National Student Association Congress, Madison, WI, August 23, 1965). http://www2.mnhs.org/library/findaids/00442/pdfa/00442-01668.pdf.

hope. Adults with an agenda may even promote the young poet or activist, featuring her at rallies, arranging book deals, and securing magazine covers. Her exuberance or ability to charm the media is mistaken for wisdom.

Fortunately, that kind of manufactured hype doesn't last. The shooting star flames out because she hasn't earned her own right to say what needs to be said.

Other examples of advice that doesn't get traction or respect may hit closer to home. If you're a parent, you've earned the right to give advice and not be disrespected. But if you've ever given driving lessons to your son or daughter, you know it doesn't always work that way. You thoughtfully lay out the rules of the road. Motivated by fear and experience, you give reasonable warnings and specific instructions. But the kid behind the wheel still grunts and delivers a world-class eye roll even as the vehicle runs the stop sign or jumps the curb. Somehow you get blamed.

Specific reasons your words of wisdom may not be heard include a disconnect with your audience or your voice being drowned out by a passing parade, a smooth-talking con artist, or a provocative whisper. If you're a baby boomer or Gen Xer, you really can't blame the millennials or Gen Z for ignoring your antiquated recommendations. Flipping that around, boomers are increasingly exasperated with younger generations who seem to speak an entirely different language and often downplay the complexity of technology insisting that, "It's really easy," when clearly, it's not.

Or maybe no one is listening because your breakthrough idea has not been tested or you haven't gained enough credibility with your intended audience.

STRATEGIES FOR GETTING YOUR VOICE HEARD

LISTEN FIRST

Ask questions to uncover the deepest needs and goals of your target audience.

IDENTIFY THEIR GOALS

Decide what your audience really wants. It may not be what's written on their placards or vocalized with their bullhorns. Most people really want the same thing: love, respect, security, and to be part of something that really matters.

FIND EVIDENCE THAT SUPPORTS YOUR IDEA

That evidence may include case studies, irrefutable data, and changed lives—including your own.

RECRUIT ALLIES

Find relatable people who can support and champion your idea. Not so you and your allies can be louder but so, together, you can offer even more love and understanding.

COME DOWN FROM YOUR SOAPBOX

Make personal connections. A little humility goes a long way. Walking alongside your enemy or someone who needs a friend can make a connection for them and provide perspective for you.

PRESENT YOUR IDEAS WITH KINDNESS AND COURTESY

Screaming gets you attention for a moment, but it will never influence anyone to think or act differently.

Not surprisingly, these strategies can be found throughout Scripture and reflected in the lives of Jesus and His followers. A few more helpful passages suggest that dispensing advice for making the world a better place is best done with grace, gentleness, and respect, and backed up by your actions.

> *Gracious words are a honeycomb, sweet to the soul and healing to the bones.* (Proverbs 16:24)

> *Always be prepared to give an answer to everyone who asks you to give the reason for the hope that you have. But do this with gentleness and respect.* (1 Peter 3:15)

> *Do not let any unwholesome talk come out of your mouths, but only what is helpful for building others up according to their needs, that it may benefit those who listen.* (Ephesians 4:29)

I have a feeling your most profound thoughts and advice are nothing to sneeze at. But you won't check many boxes until you have earned the right to be heard.

☑ CHECKING THE BOX

If you're an authentic follower of Christ, heed the advice above. Unless, of course, the earlier chapters in this book have not earned this author the right to share his opinion. See what I did there?

TO PONDER OR SHARE...

☐ 1. How do you respond to someone who hasn't earned the right to speak into your life or give you advice?

☐ 2. Do you know someone who has great ideas but fails to listen and build consensus? Does that describe you?

☐ 3. Although generalities are dangerous, how do members of your generation typically express their opinion?

☐ 4. What's your current soapbox issue? Who is and isn't listening?

☐ 5. Can you see how this chapter applies to sharing the gospel with "gentleness and respect"?

16

THINK GENERATIONALLY

"Once thoroughly broken down,
who is he that can repair the damage?"[29]
—Frederick Douglass

If you're a parent, raising your children to be respectful, productive, and heavenly minded may be your most important box to check. Your kids may even provide your best and most obvious chance at fulfilling the focus of this book: "to make the world a better place."

Certainly, you can still pursue any or all the other thirty-nine strategies in this book. But don't miss the opportunity you have right in front of you. That cooing bundle of joy, knee-high munchkin, or eye-rolling teenager may well be your most enduring legacy, which means your committed love and guidance is crucially needed.

What's more, as the role of family continues to be redefined, saving the planet and fulfilling the Great Commission (see Matthew 28:19–20) requires all of us to begin thinking generationally. It's essential that grandparents, aunts, uncles, older siblings, and anyone interacting with young people be more intentional when it comes to mentoring, discipleship, accountability, and love.

In many ways, the future is in your hands. The Bible famously confirms the lasting power of preemptive character building. *"Train up a child in the way he should go: and when he is old, he*

29. Frederick Douglass, *My Bondage and My Freedom*, ed. John Stauffer (n.p., n,d.), 85.

will not depart from it" (Proverbs 22:6 KJV). Let's invest a moment to dissect this beloved Proverb, phrase by phrase, and underscore three truths. Train up a child...in the way he should go...and when he is old, he will not depart from it.

First, children can and should be trained. We shouldn't let them wander recklessly through life doing whatever they happen to think is right.

Second, each child has their own God-given gifts and abilities, which suggests each young person has a unique and discoverable platform on which to build their best life.

Third, lessons learned early have staying power, so taking time to teach eternal truths has long-term value.

The verse also reminds us that children eventually make the choice to follow our training or not. We won't always be around to guide, rescue, or protect them. That's okay, because if we trained them early with intentionality, our words and example will stick.

Hint: Your training should include pursuing virtues like integrity, generosity, gratitude, gentleness, respect, diligence, and love. And avoiding things like laziness, rage, envy, racism, spite, faultfinding, and vulgarity. You can prioritize your own lists of virtues and vices, but shouldn't all of those lists have some basics that are obvious and inarguable?

If it's not clear, your actions will speak louder than your words. "Training up a child" requires our own self-awareness and self-discipline. You may have some personal baggage to unload. Even as you accept this challenge, it's quite possible you have to overcome some less-than-ideal "training up" from your own upbringing. The recommendation is to not dwell on it. You may have some work to do regarding challenges or even trauma from your past, but don't let that be an excuse. Do what it takes to look to the future, to the opportunity ahead of you. Those young people you love so much have their own boxes waiting to be checked.

KEYS FOR PASSING ALONG GENERATIONAL SUCCESS

KIDS WITH VALUES ARE PART OF THE SOLUTION

Instead of seeing children as a burden or hassle, what if we empowered them to be difference makers? Parents who whine about how life is unfair or cast aspersions on their offspring are setting those kids up for failure. Don't raise victims, raise change agents, and equip them to be a voice of reason.

LEADERS DON'T HAPPEN BY ACCIDENT

Tomorrow's leaders will require critical thinking skills, courage, and a sense of justice and compassion. That means adults in their lives need to provide opportunities for them to experience triumphs and endure disappointments. The result will be sons and daughters with resilience, humility, problem-solving skills, and an eternal worldview.

BE AN EXAMPLE

Modeling has always been a more effective teaching tool than lecturing. If you do feel the need to lecture the next generation, first model the lifestyle and lesson you want them to learn.

THE POSITIVES OF PEER PRESSURE

Middle school self-esteem courses label peer pressure as an evil, but they are missing the point. During some seasons of childhood, friends have more impact on a child than any other relationships. Kids who learn kindness, generosity, respect, and faith early will spread those values to peers who may never learn them at home.

INVESTING IN YOUNG PEOPLE GENERATES HOPE

As the world becomes smaller, the impact of the next generation increases. Adults may blow our own chance to make the world a better place, but our children can still carry that torch.

The Bible affirms that parents not only need to love God wholeheartedly but also make it part of their daily routine to instill that value into the next generation. *"Love the* LORD *your God with all your heart and with all your soul and with all your strength. These commandments that I give you today are to be on your hearts. Impress them on your children. Talk about them when you sit at home and when you walk along the road, when you lie down and when you get up"* (Deuteronomy 6:5–7).

☑ CHECKING THE BOX

Guilt should not be the primary motivation for wanting to leave the world a better place. Still, after we're gone, we don't want our kids (or their kids) to say, "Who are the selfish jerks who left us this mess?" With that in mind, let's all pledge to be positive examples for the next generation and leave them with resources, training, inspiration, and confidence to be all they can be.

TO PONDER OR SHARE...

☐ 1. How are the children in your life doing? Are you doing your part to give them a solid life foundation?

☐ 2. Who or what has the biggest influence on the children you know?

☐ 3. What life skills and virtues are you especially eager to pass on to the next generation?

☐ 4. What occasions referenced in Deuteronomy 6:5–7 provide the best opportunity to "impress" God's commandments on children?

☐ 5. Will you more likely impact the next generation with words or actions?

17

WELCOME SECOND CHANCES

"There's nothing as exciting as a comeback—
seeing someone with dreams, watching them fail, and then
getting a second chance."[30]
—Rachel Griffiths

We all mess up. I know I do. And I have a sneaking suspicion you do as well. Sometimes it's nothing. Typos in a text. Forgetting a name. Wearing socks with sandals. Burning a batch of cookies. An occasional minor faux pas that we can laugh about later just means we're human.

But sometimes a stumble has longer-lasting implications. Something said in anger scars a relationship. A minor error in judgment results in an almost irreversible loss or injury. A broken law. A broken trust. A broken vow. You can apologize—and you should—but sometimes you can't take it back. The damage is done. The residual impact endures, and the wounded party holds the key to your chance at a fresh start or a restored relationship.

Gotta love second chances. A heartfelt and openhanded second chance can be even more soul-satisfying than receiving forgiveness. The act of forgiving can release negative emotions and even remove resentment. But a second chance provides an opportunity

---

30. "Rachel Griffiths Quotes," Brainy Quote, accessed March 18, 2024, https://www.brainyquote.com/quotes/rachel_griffiths_238605.

for complete redemption. You might even think of it as a reset, a fresh start, or a do-over.

In a friendly game, golfers might allow their opponents a mulligan. In the 1993 dark comedy *Groundhog Day*, Bill Murray's character doesn't realize it initially, but he gets hundreds of do-overs on that fateful day in Punxsutawney, Pennsylvania, until he finally gets it right. In real life, second chances seem to go against human nature here in the 21st century.

Accepting a second chance requires you to admit how you messed up, but more than that, it means taking additional steps to make things right and to make sure it doesn't happen again. By the way, that can never happen if you enter into denial, make excuses, blame someone else, get angry, or hide the evidence hoping no one ever finds out about it.

Even better than *getting* a second chance is *giving* one. That heroic gesture might begin on your part by confirming, "You are forgiven," but it goes beyond. It's welcoming the offender back into your life and restoring your relationship to its former status. You may be tempted to establish boundaries or lay out conditions for your renewed relationship. But, if possible, give the gift of offering a truly clean slate with no strings attached.

The first murder ever was the result of Cain ignoring, or perhaps refusing, a second chance offered by God Himself. Most people don't remember that part of the story from Genesis 4:5–7. After his sacrifice is rejected, Cain is angry, but that's not what prompts him to kill his brother Abel. What really ticks off Cain is that God gives him a fresh chance to make things right and even spells out the consequences if he doesn't: "*You will be accepted if you do what is right. But if you refuse to do what is right, then watch out! Sin is crouching at the door, eager to control you. But you must subdue it and be its master*" (Genesis 4:7 NLT).

We're not told why, but Cain doesn't take the do-over option. He kills Abel, denies responsibility, loses the ability to grow crops, and is banished to wander the earth away from the presence of the Lord.

Such is the critical nature of a second chance. If it's offered, take it. If at all possible, give one to that person who grieved you. The world will be a better place because you checked that box.

THE UPSIDE OF A FRESH START

A SECOND CHANCE CAN RESCUE AN ORGANIZATION

Ousted from the company he had helped to create, Steve Jobs later returned to Apple in 1997, introducing a string of world-changing products.

A SECOND CHANCE CAN TRANSFORM A VILLAGE

Jesus spoke truth into the life of the Samaritan woman at the well. (See John 4.) Renewed by the encounter, back in her village, her word was trusted and many were redeemed.

A SECOND CHANCE CAN RESET A MISSION

Jonah refused his assignment and was thrown overboard. Once vomited ashore by the big fish, Jonah took his second chance to go to Nineveh and lead that city to its own repentance and second chance. Jonah 3:10 records, *"When God saw what they did and how they turned from their evil ways, he relented and did not bring on them the destruction he had threatened."*

A SECOND CHANCE DEEPENS RELATIONSHIPS

Since we all mess up, we all appreciate a fresh start. More than that, overcoming a division between friends, colleagues, classmates, or family members often forges a bond that lasts a lifetime.

It's been said that "Christians have a God of second chances." That's good news because even those who understand and have accepted Jesus and God's free gift of grace are still going to sin.

Such is our fallen human nature. What's more, as we are made in God's image, we might also embrace the practice of giving second chances.

☑ CHECKING THE BOX

> If someone wrongs you, be eager to forgive. And if possible, model God's promise to cast that transgression far away and out of sight. It takes a special kind of love—a kind of love that follows God's example—but it's worth the effort: *"For as high as the heavens are above the earth, so great is his love for those who fear him; as far as the east is from the west, so far has he removed our transgressions from us"* (Psalm 103:11–12).

TO PONDER OR SHARE...

☐ 1. You knew the story of Cain and Abel, but did you recall that God gave Cain a fresh chance to turn away from sin?

☐ 2. We can't forgive as God forgives. Or can we?

☐ 3. How is forgiveness different from a second chance?

☐ 4. Have you given or been given a second chance?

☐ 5. How do you interpret the adage, "Christians have a God of second chances"?

18

IDENTIFY LONELINESS

"Yes, there is joy, fulfillment and companionship—but the loneliness of the soul in its appalling self-consciousness is horrible and overpowering."[31]
—Sylvia Plath

How is it possible to feel alone in a crowded room? Have you ever wondered if your friends were really your friends? Or maybe you've thought, "No one knows me. No one really cares. No one would miss me if I wasn't here. I might as well be invisible."

Before you get lost in too deep of a funk, please know that most of us have been there. We enter an empty room and turn on the TV for company. We feel alone as we ride a crowded elevator among strangers. On a street corner, faceless crowds scurry past and we stand immobilized and isolated amidst the blur of activity.

If all this leaves you feeling lost in the cold, there are three things you need to consider.

First, you're never alone. The last words in the Gospel of Matthew are Jesus's promise to His followers, *"And surely I am with you always, to the very end of the age"* (Matthew 28:20). That's always worth remembering, especially during those times when our human friends have ditched us.

---

31. Sylvia Plath, *The Journals of Sylvia Plath* (New York: Anchor Books, 1998), 19.

Second, there are dozens of things you can do this week to engage with others and combat your own loneliness, some easier or more obvious than others. You can volunteer. Visit an old friend. Join a club. Join a small group. Join a book club. Begin a new hobby. Go to the gym. Make amends with an old adversary. Walk around the block. Wave at neighbors. Be a regular at a coffee shop. Plant a plot at a community vegetable garden. Adopt a pet. Go to the dog park. Enroll in an off-the-wall class at the local community college. Set up an easel and paint a local landmark. Attend (or perform) in a freestyle poetry jam. Do chalk art in the park. Paint small rocks with encouraging phrases and leave them in public spaces. Become a foster parent. Revisit a hobby or interest from years ago. Find the lowest roundtrip airfare to any city and book a long weekend. Go to a library, park, or community center and pick up a brochure. Sit on one side of a park bench. Buy a snowblower and clear your neighbor's sidewalk. Start a small business.

You'll notice that none of these box-checking ideas involve engaging with others solely via telephone or video. For most of us, being in the same space and breathing the same air—if possible—is a more promising remedy for feelings of loneliness.

Third, realize that—even if you're not lonely—there are scores of others in your community who are. As someone who cares about the world, go ahead and take any of the above ideas and seize the opportunity. While you're changing the world for someone else, you might also brighten your own corner of the world.

RESPONSES TO LONELINESS

DON'T CONFUSE LONELINESS WITH SOLITUDE

Solitude can be a powerful force for good. The Bible tells us that even Jesus would often slip away to the wilderness for some time alone. *"But Jesus often withdrew to lonely places and prayed"* (Luke 5:16).

LONELINESS IS ON THE RISE

A recent report by the U.S. Surgeon General described an "epidemic of loneliness and isolation" resulting in a 29 percent increased risk of heart disease, a 32 percent increased risk of stroke, and a 50 percent increased risk of developing dementia for older adults. In addition to that, lack of social connection increases the risk of premature death by more than 60 percent.[32]

IT TAKES COURAGE TO PUT YOURSELF OUT THERE

Joining an established group or trying something slightly daring is really difficult for some people. If that describes your current mindset, ask yourself, "What's the worst that could happen?"

Identifying and responding to loneliness might be one of the most loving and valuable boxes you could ever check. With the breakup of the family, mental health issues, language barriers, cyber seclusion, economic insecurity, workplace trends, and so many other issues, social isolation has reached crisis level. You know someone—maybe an older member of your extended family—currently facing a season of desperate loneliness, don't you?

☑ CHECKING THE BOX

Humans were made for community. Each of us has gifts that are meant to be shared and enjoyed. That means walking across a room, knocking on a door, or striking up a conversation with a stranger. Being aware of loneliness is a skill you can develop and a gift you can give humanity.

32. "New Surgeon General Advisory Raises Alarm about the Devastating Impact of the Epidemic of Loneliness and Isolation in the United States," U. S. Department of Health and Human Services, May 3, 2023, https://www.hhs.gov/about/news/2023/05/03/new-surgeon-general-advisory-raises-alarm-about-devastating-impact-epidemic-loneliness-isolation-united-states.html.

TO PONDER OR SHARE...

☐ 1. What are the benefits of being alone? What are the drawbacks?

☐ 2. What are three activities that might lead to more human engagement for you? (Review the long list above.)

☐ 3. When's the last time you "put yourself out there"? What's holding you back?

☐ 4. Who do you know that might be lonely? (Consider relatives, friends, neighbors, and coworkers, both past and present.)

☐ 5. When you engage others, what are specific ways you can foster joy and positivity in their lives?

19

UNKNOWINGLY INSPIRE

"Words are, of course, the most powerful drug used by mankind."
—Rudyard Kipling[33]

When I was in third grade, my parents came home from a parent-teacher conference and relayed to me something Mrs. Colby had told them. She said, "Jay doesn't really say much in class discussion, but when he does, it's worth listening to."[34]

I liked that. Now, decades later, I realize that brief remark might be the cornerstone of my writing and speaking career. *Make it relevant. Keep it short.*

That idea served me well in the decade I spent on Michigan Avenue in Chicago, as a copywriter crafting short-and-sweet ads for Midway Airlines, Veg-All, Corona beer, and the Chicago Symphony Orchestra. Succinct relevance is also the secret to the thousands of radio scripts I've written for ministries such as The Voice of the Martyrs, National Center for Fathering, The Salvation Army, and Museum of the Bible. Short chapters are the building blocks to most of my more than thirty books, including this one.

---

33. Rudyard Kipling, "Surgeons and the Soul" (speech, Annual Dinner of the Royal College of Surgeons, Lincoln's Inn, February 14, 1923), https://www.telelib.com/words/authors/K/KiplingRudyard/prose/BookOfWords/surgeonssoul.html.
34. This chapter adapted in part from Jay Payleitner, What If God Wrote Your To-Do List? (Eugene, OR: Harvest House Publishers, 2018), 47.

All that to say, brief positive words spoken by a person I respected have had a long-lasting impact on my life. Still, I'm quite sure Mrs. Colby had no idea of the significant impact her words would make. But it's a wonderful example of Proverbs 25:11: *"A word fitly spoken is like apples of gold in settings of silver"* (NKJV).

A more world-changing example comes from the life of Dwight L. Moody, founder of the Moody Bible Institute in Chicago, and perhaps the greatest evangelist of the nineteenth century. Before broadcasting and social media, Moody preached the gospel to more than 100 million people in tents, church buildings, town squares, and battlefields across Europe and America.

An inspiring quote often attributed to Moody is one he would emphatically confirm was spoken by another man. It was British revivalist Henry Varley who said, "The world has yet to see what God can do with a man fully consecrated to Him."

Varley spoke those words in a private conversation to his new friend D. L. Moody during an 1872 revivalist crusade in Dublin. Moody took that one-sentence challenge to heart, and it motivated his ministry for the rest of his life. A year later, Moody would tell Varley,

> "Those were the words sent to my soul, through you from the living God. As I crossed the wide Atlantic the boards of the deck of the vessel were engraved with them, and when I reached Chicago the very paving stones seemed marked with 'Moody, the world has yet to see what God will do with a man fully consecrated to him.' Under the power of those words I have come back to England, and I felt that I must not let more time pass until I let you know how God had used your words to my inmost soul."[35]

Varley was touched and honored to have been used by God in that way. But—and here's the takeaway for all of us—Varley

<hr>

35. Cited in A. P. Fitt, ed., *The Institute Tie*, volume 3 (September 1902 to August 1903), 122.

did not recall speaking that life-changing quote to his friend. He told Moody, "I well remember our interview, but I do not recall any special utterance."

That's right. Henry Varley could not recall saying the most inspiring and constructive words ever to come out of his mouth.

And maybe, neither will you. Over the course of your life, you will have the chance to speak into the lives of hundreds, perhaps thousands, of individuals. Children who need to feel special. Teenagers making life-changing decisions. Young adults considering careers and ministries. That might include your own children, grandchildren, nieces, and nephews. Students, mentees, young athletes, or neighbor kids. Or maybe someone from the next generation with whom you happen to cross paths in a single afternoon or moment in time.

Active in my own church over the years, I can remember two quietly thrilling moments that took me by surprise. For a few years, baptism services included a recorded testimony played for the congregation moments before each baptism. Two times my name came up as part of someone's testimony—once from a member of my small group, and once from a boy who had been part of my middle school huddle. I had no idea the words I'd spoken had impacted their lives so much.

I'm not taking credit here. The point is that each one of us has the chance to check this box and begin discerning and praising the innate gifts of the people whose paths we cross. Our words spoken into the lives of individuals—like ripples in a pond—can touch the hearts and minds of countless people.

USEFUL TIPS TO HELP INSPIRE

INSPIRING WORDS ARE PERSONAL

You likely have heard first-person accounts of people recalling how a few words changed the course of their life or career. In almost every case, those were private or personal words not broadcast to the world but spoken heart to heart.

ESCHEW FALSE PRAISE

Hollow compliments and flattery motivated by self-interest yield the reverse outcome. Artificial accolades leave a trail of failure, disappointment, and broken trust. *"To flatter friends is to lay a trap for their feet"* (Proverbs 29:5 NLT).

USE SMALL WORDS

Bombastic praise rings hollow. But simple, sincere words will penetrate hearts. "Your kindness touches me." "You have a gift and God's going to use it." "Your optimism is a ray of sunshine."

USE SCRIPTURE

If you're not good with words, borrow God's. "I appreciate how you are quick to listen and slow to speak." "You are such an encouragement!" "Your calming presence means so much to me." (See James 1:19, Romans 12:7–8, and Psalm 37:7.)

If you're open to the Spirit while grounded in reality, there's a good chance you will have a weekly opportunity to speak inspiration into the life of a family member, friend, or stranger. God uses faithful believers to deliver his love and encouragement to the world—sometimes in auditoriums and cathedrals, but more often, one person at a time.

☑ CHECKING THE BOX

> You may never know how your words impact the trajectory of another person's life. Like my third-grade teacher in the suburbs of Chicago or Henry Varley in Dublin, keep listening, caring, and doing God's work. Occasionally, let God speak through your voice, and without even knowing it, you may change a life or change history.

TO PONDER OR SHARE...

☐ 1. Who has helped you see your giftedness? What did they say? How can you thank them today?

☐ 2. This chapter is titled, "Unknowingly Inspire," and you can do that simply by offering encouraging words or pointing out achievements that may have been overlooked. But what if you were even more purposeful in identifying and celebrating the gifts of others?

☐ 3. When highlighting the gifts of others, how important is sincerity? Is it sometimes okay to just make stuff up?

☐ 4. In your family or circle of friends, who might benefit from your short and sincere recognition of their giftedness?

☐ 5. Does this challenge to inspire others apply solely to people you know well, or does it extend to strangers you might meet?

20

STICK TO THE RULES

"We cannot break the Ten Commandments. We can only
break ourselves against them."[36]
—Cecil B. DeMille

Back in chapter eleven, we endorsed the value of the fifth commandment, which is pretty much a no-brainer. Honoring parents strengthens families, and strong families create a launchpad for individuals to make a difference in the world.

This chapter serves as a reminder that the other nine commandments God carved on stone and gave to Moses on Mount Sinai some 3,500 years ago also prove extremely valuable in our pursuit of making the world a better place. Unfortunately, much of the world—even folks who identify as Christians—don't seem too concerned about checking these boxes.

Occasionally the Ten Commandments make the news because some group labeled as religious fanatics is trying to post them in a public place. The irony is that most folks who would say they endorse the Ten Commandments probably can't recite them. Can you?

If not, feel free to put down this book and open your Bible to Exodus, chapter 20, and do a complete review of the entire list.

---

36. Cecil B. DeMille, Commencement Address (Brigham Young University, May 31, 1957), https://speeches.byu.edu/talks/cecil-b-demille/ten-commandments-and-you/.

As a helpful recap, here's a kid-friendly paraphrase taken from a poster produced several years ago by InspirationArt & Scripture:

+ Hey, there's only one God.

+ Make Him first in your life.

+ Even God's name is powerful.

+ Sunday rocks.

+ Be excellent to your mom and add.

+ Don't waste your life or anyone else's.

+ Husbands and wives are made for each other.

+ Stealing is just wrong and you know it.

+ Be real! Do not lie about other people.

+ Be happy with your own stuff.

Make sense? Could you follow? Does this resemble the Ten Commandments you've come to know?

Admittedly, that kind of paraphrase might not sit well with some theological purists. That's understandable. We certainly don't want to trivialize or sugarcoat any portion of God's Word. Still, I do think it can be helpful to reframe some of the "thou shalt nots" into positive commands. In that way, for example, the sixth commandment confirms the value of respecting and protecting life, and the seventh celebrates the commitment and bond of marriage.

I hope you agree that any thoughtful analysis and application of the Ten Commandments can be beneficial. The Ten Commandments are universal and far-reaching, and they apply to just about any ethical or moral question that humans may face. Historians trace the principles embedded in the Magna Carta, the U.S. Constitution, and other governing codes back to the Ten Commandments.

It's impossible, of course, but try to imagine a world in which the moral framework as set forth in the Ten Commandments was universally taught and obeyed. The world would be a better place.

REKINDLING THE TEN COMMANDMENTS

RULES FOR YOUR FAMILY

Commandments five and seven focus on family and marriage—more specifically, how you relate to your parents and the blessings of intimacy in a committed marriage. To be clear, getting married and bearing children are not an obligation. But sleeping around and dishonoring your parents is unacceptable.

ESTABLISH BASELINE VALUES

Commandments six, eight, nine, and ten offer irrefutably good advice on murder, stealing, lying, and coveting. These are basic, logical, beneficial rules for humans. Arguably, any of these four immoral behaviors can cause life-changing damage, to your own life and any lives you touch.

REMEMBER TO REST

We can argue about commandment four and the definition of "Sabbath," but let's face it, even God rested on the seventh day. Pull your weight six days per week, then rest; be productive, then rejuvenate. Even more than that, dedicate that seventh day to the Lord for gathering with His people to worship and learn more about Him.

THERE IS A GOD

Commandments one, two, and three confirm that we can know God, that false gods are powerless, and that even God's name is powerful.

These rules were carved in stone. Twice. And there's a wonderful clarity about them. What if they really are the perfect rules for life given to us from a loving Father?

☑ CHECKING THE BOX

The Ten Commandments are not just a list of dos and don'ts. They help you keep balance in your life in every critical area, including how to relate to the Creator; how to work and rest; how to relate to other people and build your family; and how to get the most out of life and help others get the most out of theirs.

TO PONDER OR SHARE...

☐ 1. Quick: Can you recite the Ten Commandments?

☐ 2. Take your time: Can you see how the Ten Commandments are more than just a list of "thou shalt not" rules?

☐ 3. What's your favorite commandment to break?

☐ 4. What if you regularly reviewed those ancient rules for life at bedtime as a checklist for your day?

☐ 5. Is it okay to have the Ten Commandments posted in our courts or public areas?

21

GET OUT OF YOUR SILO

"Where all think alike, no one thinks very much."[37]
—Walter Lippmann

On my credenza is the *Merriam-Webster's Collegiate Dictionary, Tenth Edition*, principal copyright 1993. Before online dictionaries, I turned to it often. Now that thick red hardcover sits under a stack of other little-used reference books as a testament to progress. To be honest, I miss thumbing through that well-worn resource and making serendipitous discoveries.

Before writing this chapter, I opened my trusted Merriam-Webster and looked up the word *silo*. The two definitions from 1993 basically referred to structures: "a tall cylinder...for storing material" and "an underground structure for housing a guided missile." There was no mention of silo as metaphor for how humans interact.

Not long after, a new definition for *silo* crept into the business world. It began as a description of organizational dysfunction when different departments within a company do their own thing, neglecting to communicate or coordinate with other departments. That kind of isolation—whether intentional or not—blocks communication, hinders innovation, leads to redundancies, frustrates customers and clients, and generates jealousy and animosity within an organization.

---

37. Walter Lippmann, *The Stakes of Diplomacy* (New York: Henry Holt and Company, 1915), 51-52.

The image is stark and accurate. Even comical. You can picture a group of corporate executives bouncing around inside a hollow concrete pillar, feeling self-important but having zero awareness of anyone outside their silo. What's more, they seemingly don't care about their isolation and the damage being done.

That illustration leads us to the latest application of the word. This understanding of *silo* is primarily driven by social media, and it's not healthy. In the early days, the great online community was promoted as a way to gather in harmony, to share ideas, and to gain a better understanding of each other. That didn't last.

It turns out the vast majority of us are now choosing to hear and listen to only those people who already believe what we believe. People in our silo read the same blogs, watch the same news commentators, and attend the same rallies. We disdainfully block out those who disagree with us. As a result, we eliminate any chance of new, helpful, or relevant ideas seeping into our concrete bunker.

As proof, just consider what happens when a stance or policy that has clear consensus in one silo somehow finds its way into an opposing silo. That sound bite, quote, clip, or meme is labeled as hate speech and goes viral to others who "think like us." Instead of changing minds, the conflict escalates.

Ask any CEO who has become aware of silos and successfully demolished the divisive silo mentality. The fog lifts, ideas are exchanged, the self-imposed oppression ends, and the best ideas rise to the surface and can be implemented for the betterment of the entire organization. That sounds like a box worth checking for any company, society, family, or government.

EMBRACE A SILO-FREE LIFE

As you consider your own peer groups and spheres of influence, what will it take to smash the cultural silos that prevent communication, collaboration, and consensus?

LEAVE YOUR SILO

You may not be able to deconstruct all the silos, but you can leave your own. Be wise as you do so. Hold on to your established values as you venture out, and find motivation in your own foundation of faith and love. The fastest way to impact an adversary is to courageously enter their arena. Matthew 10:16 puts it this way: "*I am sending you out like sheep among wolves. Therefore be as shrewd as snakes and as innocent as doves.*"

MERGE SILOS

Take the best of yours and the best of a neighboring silo. Respectfully share research and successes. Separate facts from opinions. Seek out complementary capabilities. Streamline and refine.

KNOW THINE ENEMY

Leave your silo as a scout. Determine whether the adversary in the opposing silo is actually an ally or a devotee of the enemy. Return with information that makes your organization—or your personal faith—stronger.

DOUBLECHECK YOUR OWN ASSERTIONS

Be wary if you find yourself saying, "Everyone agrees...," or "Studies have shown...," or "I'm one 100 percent sure that...." Those all sound like silo speak.

Christians need to hold tight to key tenets of the faith. The list is worth reviewing: God as omnipotent Creator. The trustworthiness of the Bible. The fact that all have sinned. Jesus's sacrifice on the cross as a free gift that paid the penalty for our sins, giving believers a home with Him in eternity. The indwelling of the Holy Spirit. There are other precepts, but you get the idea. (Please note: If someone in another silo believes what you believe, they could very well be an ally, not an enemy; they are worth listening to.)

☑ CHECKING THE BOX

As you engage with others, you should regularly find yourself thinking, "I hadn't considered that perspective before." Romans 12:16 (NLT) confirms the need to listen, live, and learn with others: *"Live in harmony with each other. Don't be too proud to enjoy the company of ordinary people. And don't think you know it all!"*

TO PONDER OR SHARE...

☐ 1. What defines your silo? Who else is in it?

☐ 2. In which of your groups might you find diverse thoughts and opinions that lead to thoughtful discussion and healthy debate?

☐ 3. When are silos—perhaps temporary silos—a good thing?

☐ 4. Does social media dismantle or reinforce silos?

☐ 5. When is the last time you allowed one of your long-held beliefs to be challenged? Did you defend your belief without reasonable deliberation? Or did you consider changing your way of thinking?

22

KNOW RIGHT FROM WRONG

"Be brave to stand up for what you truly believe in even if you stand alone."[38]
—Roy T. Bennett

I have identified a bunch of absolutes in my life—things I believe are right, and things I believe are wrong. I suspect you've probably done the same. I also suspect most of our absolutes may overlap.

Let's list a few. Because it's easy, let's begin with some things that are undeniably wrong: Murder. Human trafficking. Adultery. Rape. Slavery. Incest. Stealing. Torture. Environmental destruction. Envy.

Are we in agreement? Are those boxes we should all be checking? It's easy to nod your head at the first six items. But what about the last four? Stealing, torture, and so on.

Anyone who's ever read or seen *Les Misérables* would agree that Jean Valjean didn't deserve his nineteen-year prison sentence for stealing bread to feed his sister's starving children. We also probably agree that torture is unacceptable—that is unless we're watching a spy thriller and the good guys have less than a minute to get a bad guy to reveal the code that will deactivate a nuclear bomb about to kill 50 million people. What about environmental

---

38. Roy T. Bennett, *The Light in the Heart: Inspirational Thoughts for Living Your Best Life* (n.p.: privately printed, 2021), 83.

destruction? Some might call Mount Rushmore, the Hoover Dam, or wind turbines destructive to the environment. Do you agree?

Finally, on a personal level, let's examine envy. If I'm honest, a dose of envy, along with my desire to give nice things to my family, has fueled my somewhat selfish motivation for writing books and speaking nationally on issues like marriage, family, and getting life right. I'm not proud of being envious, but the results have actually helped make the world a better place, I think.

Labeling things "the right things to do" has a complicated history. All you have to do is look at the Bill of Rights, which has largely stood the test of time, to see what I mean. Here's a partial list of rights as outlined in the first ten amendments: freedom of religion, freedom of speech, freedom of the press, freedom of assembly, the right to keep and bear arms, freedom from unreasonable searches and seizures, the right to due process and a speedy trial by your peers, and freedom from cruel and unusual punishment.

Are there gray areas here? Of course, and that's why the justice system exists, because even these "good rights" can be twisted and used for bad. Free speech can threaten, incite, and even turn deadly. Assembly can sometimes turn into mob action. I can think of a few people who should not be allowed to carry a gun. And who determines the definition of words like *unreasonable, speedy, cruel,* and *unusual?* The fact that the U.S. Constitution brilliantly includes a built-in methodology for being amended confirms that "right" and "wrong" may be difficult to ascertain at any given moment for any given quandary.

So how can an individual ever determine right from wrong? Can there really be any absolutes when it comes to ethical clarity? The answer is yes. Stay with me now.

There is an absolute measurement for what time it is. Back in 1884, an international convention determined the clock at the Royal Observatory in Greenwich, London, would be the standard for the world. Not surprisingly, the original motivation for setting a universal benchmark was to synchronize rail travel. Satellites and digital communication might seem to make the Shepherd Gate Clock at the observatory obsolete. Still, if you want to know the exact right time, Greenwich sets the standard.

In the same way, the International Bureau of Weights and Measures in Saint-Cloud, France, literally has a perfect liter and a perfect meter on-site that are considered the definitive standards for measuring volume and length. If you want to know for sure that your bottle of ginger ale is exactly one liter, head to France and compare it to that faultless model.

Wouldn't it be nice to have an equally handy benchmark for right and wrong? An infallible measure. A flawless standard by which we can compare our decisions and actions. Is that possible?

I hope you know where this is going. In any case, allow me to spell it out. The Creator of the universe has set forth an entire system of absolutes. God has, indeed, provided exemplary standards. It will take some study and some level of trust, but if we really want to make the world a better place, doing the right thing as determined by God and as modeled by Jesus is the right place to start. That needs to be our baseline.

Here's how this idea plays out. God is life, so we need to honor the life of every person. God is truth, so we need to be honest even when the truth hurts. God is just, so we need to play fair. God is mercy, so we are called to live without shame and be eager to forgive. God is righteous, so our goal is to act with integrity and to live honorably.[39]

ALIGNING WITH GOD'S PRECEPTS

Dare we compare ourselves to God? Yes! As humans, we will undeniably fall way short. But His standard is the goal. The result

---

39. For a further discussion on these ideas, please see Josh McDowell and Bob Hostetler, *Right from Wrong* (Dallas: Word Publishing, 1994), 94–99.

is a better world. In our goal to make the world a better place, here are a few of God's rules that elevate others.

BE A HELP

"*Carry each other's burdens, and in this way you will fulfill the law of Christ*" (Galatians 6:2).

GIVE OF YOURSELF

"*Do not forget to do good and to share with others, for with such sacrifices God is pleased*" (Hebrews 13:16).

BE GENEROUS

"*Give to the one who asks you, and do not turn away from the one who wants to borrow from you*" (Matthew 5:42).

WELCOME STRANGERS

"*Share with the Lord's people who are in need. Practice hospitality*" (Romans 12:13).

BE SELFLESS

"*Heal the sick, raise the dead, cleanse those who have leprosy, drive out demons. Freely you have received; freely give*" (Matthew 10:8).

INSPIRE

"*Encourage one another and build each other up, just as in fact you are doing*" (1 Thessalonians 5:11).

FEED THE HUNGRY

"*Spend yourselves in behalf of the hungry and satisfy the needs of the oppressed, then your light will rise in the darkness, and your night will become like the noonday*" (Isaiah 58:10).

KEEP YOUR EYES OPEN TO THE NEEDS OF OTHERS

"*Learn to do right; seek justice. Defend the oppressed. Take up the cause of the fatherless; plead the case of the widow*" (Isaiah 1:17).

☑ CHECKING THE BOX

Never let anyone claim there is no right or wrong. The idea that what's wrong for one person is okay for someone else goes against the very character of God, who is unchanging and eternal. Psalm 100:5 confirms, *"The LORD is good and his love endures forever; his faithfulness continues through all generations."* We can't expect to get it right all the time, but whenever someone chooses to know and pursue godly standards, the world becomes ever so much better.

TO PONDER OR SHARE...

☐ 1. Can you list your absolutes? Should those also be your neighbor's absolutes?

☐ 2. How do you respond to the statements, "What's true for you may not be true for me" or "Don't impose your values on me"?

☐ 3. Who or what better determines right and wrong: personal conscience, cultural norms, logic, God's character, school boards, parents, peers, the United Nations, laws established by your own government, or something else?

☐ 4. Which of the Ten Commandments has the most gray area?

☐ 5. How can understanding the character of God make the world a better place?

23

CALL THEIR NAMES

"Remember that a person's name is to that person the sweetest and most important sound in any language."[40]
—Dale Carnegie

In the parable of the good shepherd, the sheep know Jesus's voice. That's not surprising. But what *is* surprising is that He calls them by name.

> *The one who enters by the gate is the shepherd of the sheep. The gatekeeper opens the gate for him, and the sheep listen to his voice. He calls his own sheep by name and leads them out.* (John 10:2–3)

Do sheep have names? Perhaps two thousand years ago they did. On my journey to Ireland with my bride a few years back, I recall hillside pastures covered with hundreds of sheep, and there's no way each had a name. On the other hand, the parable is not really about domesticated fleecy livestock. It's about those who choose to follow Jesus and how He cares for them.

As an authentic Christian, you can be sure Jesus knows your name. And everything else about you.

---

40. Dale Carnegie, *How to Win Friends & Influence People* (New York: Simon & Schuster, 1936; New York: Pocket Books, a division of Simon & Schuster, 1981), citation to the 1981 edition, 105.

I think this parable also confirms that names matter. I'm reminded of the summer our church finally hired our first full-time youth pastor. Frank, a new graduate of Wheaton College, set his sights on preparing for the upcoming school year. You might think his objectives would have been obvious. Priorities for the summer would certainly be getting to know the rest of the ministry staff, preparing curriculum, recruiting volunteers, and planning a youth-friendly event to kick off the ministry year.

Frank did all that. But he identified and executed another task that was much more critical. He gathered the names of every high school student who was connected in any way to our church, and he prayed. He prayed for each of them by name, every day, for the entire summer.

What did that accomplish? Those prayers softened Frank's heart for each of those young people. Also, without them even knowing it, the heart of each student was being prepared to hear the gospel and the biblical truth that they all desperately needed. And who knows? Those heartfelt prayers that summer may have helped more than one teen deal effectively with a personal crisis or difficult decision. Frank's prayers may have prevented one parent from losing their cool and kicking their son out of the house after a two-way screaming match that got out of hand. That summer of intentional prayer may have prevented one kid from drinking, another kid from smoking pot, and a young couple from giving into temptation and losing their virginity. That's all very possible.

What's more, near the end of summer, scores of students found themselves inexplicably drawn to the first-ever youth group kick-off event. And guess what? The new youth pastor already knew their names. They came back, and they got curious about Jesus.

Names matter. Those young people felt loved, respected, and personally connected to the youth pastor and, subsequently, to the youth group, the church, and God. I saw it happen to Eric, Becky, Brad, Amy, Sarah, Tony, Sheila, and many of the other 150 names that were prayed for *by name* all summer long. These were real kids with real needs.

In much the same way, we need to see our neighbors and all the people of the world as individuals. It's probably okay to think of "people groups" and even discuss the culture and needs of various demographics in terms of language, customs, and traditions. However, when we find ourselves applying stereotypes or prejudices, then we need to take a step back and examine our own hearts and motivations. To check this box, we need to embrace the idea that every individual has their own gifts and holds inherent worth in the eyes of God. Each person has infinite value. Each person has their own name.

GOD'S INVALUABLE HUMAN CREATION

PEOPLE LOVE THE SOUND OF THEIR NAME

Neuroscience confirms that portions of the brain—the middle frontal cortex, cuneus, and other parts of the left hemisphere—spring to life when a person hears their name spoken aloud.[41]

USING NAMES LEADS TO FRIENDSHIPS

Recall a conversation with a stranger. On a plane, in a line, at a sporting event or concert. After talking for a while, they reach out their hand and say their name. "I'm Melanie." "I'm Leo." That handshake and that permission to use their name changes everything. (Side note: As the conversation continues, use that name, and you may now have a new friend.)

BELIEF IN YOUR OWN VALUE FUELS ACHIEVEMENT

In conversation, using names in an affirming way and seeing people as individuals empowers them to take personal responsibility for their own needs and actions.

---

41. Dennis Carmody and Michael Lewis, "Brain activation when hearing one's own and others' names," *Brain Research* 1116, no. 1 (2006): 153–158, https://doi.org/10.1016/j.brainres.2006.07.121.

INDIVIDUALS CHOOSE TO FOLLOW CHRIST ONE AT A TIME

Families, tribes, and countries might be labeled as "Christian," but that doesn't mean everyone in that group is secure in their faith. America's history, the founding documents, and the belief system of a majority of its citizens are rooted in Christianity. Still, having a street address in one of the fifty states doesn't make you a follower of Christ. Individuals have to make their own decision to accept the free gift of grace.

As individuals we are called, each in turn, by name. Isaiah 43:1 confirms, "*Do not fear, for I have redeemed you; I have summoned you by name; you are mine.*" That biblical principle should help us see strangers and people from other cultures as individuals loved by God.

☑ CHECKING THE BOX

If you haven't yet realized it, this book is not really about transforming the world into a utopia of perfection. It's about identifying core principles that individuals—each of whom have a name—need to understand and embrace. Will all eight billion inhabitants of the planet do that? Probably not. But that doesn't mean we shouldn't try. In the meantime, there are people whose names you know who need Jesus in their life. Start there.

TO PONDER OR SHARE...

☐ 1. Do you have a hard time remembering peoples' names? Seek out techniques and tricks to get better at that important skill!

☐ 2. Do you pray for people by name? (That will help your memory!)

☐ 3. Of the eight billion citizens of earth, which ones are you responsible for?

☐ 4. Do you hang on to stereotypes? Or do you recognize how each individual has needs and abilities?

☐ 5. Is your name written in the book of life? (See Revelation 20:15.)

24

FEED YOUR ENEMY

I always forgive my enemies; nothing enrages them more.[42]
—Felix Grendon

According to my own unofficial poll, half the people on earth are your enemy[43]. Everything they believe is the complete opposite of what you stand for. Their politics, religion, sexual preference, parenting style, and worldview are ridiculous, evil, and/or delusional.

Upon further review, it may not be exactly fifty-fifty, but there are most definitely two (or more) sides to any debate on creationism, climate change, vaccinations, alternative medicine, border security, gun control, gender equality, euthanasia, right to life, censorship, religious freedom, wealth redistribution, defense spending, GMOs, animal rights, and flat earth theory.

You may hold your beliefs firmly and quietly or be an outspoken warrior. You may be itching for a fight or seeking a peaceful coexistence. Many people I know are desperately trying to figure out how to get someone they love to jump ship and join their team.

This chapter will not attempt to take any particular stance in any of these particular debates. Instead, let's consider the most

---

42. Felix Grendon, "The Cool Philosopher" *The International* IV, no. 6 (November 1911), 90.
43. Please note: In this short chapter, the word "enemy" is not referring to Satan. We're talking about folks who have a heart, conscience, capacity to love, and potential for change.

effective way to interact with our enemies so that we can live next door, work together, serve with one another on PTO, or sit next to each other at a Thanksgiving table in peace. (And maybe get them to consider switching sides.)

Our first instinct is to weaponize ourselves. Recruit an army. Bolster our arguments. Use the power of words to outsmart, out-yell, defame, manipulate, gaslight, spread rumors, harass, victim shame, demean, threaten, and all those verbal strategies that are so popular in social media and during not-so-peaceful demonstrations and marches.

If you've been on the receiving end of hurtful words—belittled, assaulted, ridiculed, mocked, scorned, bullied, ostracized, or harassed —it's human nature to fight back with your own hate-filled response. Yes, it's natural. But it's also wrong. To properly and effectively check this box, we need a *supernatural* response.

In our own power, there's no way we can live up to the command, *"Love your enemies and pray for those who persecute you"* (Matthew 5:44). Does this clear command sound impossible? It is for nonbelievers. But for those who trust God, we have a supernatural resource we can count on. Guided by the Holy Spirit, we can actually love our persecutors in the same way God loves them. We can pray for them, because we know God's intervention really can soften their hearts—and ours.

Beyond that, two biblical principles make the idea of loving your enemies a little more manageable.

First, be assured your enemies are not "getting away" with anything. They will have to settle up with God for any of their sinful behavior at a later date.

Second, there is a way to utilize their malevolent nature to turn their life around. Since you are in direct contact with them, you just might be the right person for the job. The strategy, as described in Romans, is this: kill 'em with kindness.

Do not repay anyone evil for evil. Be careful to do what is right in the eyes of everyone. If it is possible, as far as it depends on you, live at peace with everyone. Do not take revenge, my dear friends, but leave room for God's wrath, for it is written: "It is mine to avenge; I will repay," says the Lord. On the contrary: "If your enemy is hungry, feed him; if he is thirsty, give him something to drink. In doing this, you will heap burning coals on his head." Do not be overcome by evil, but overcome evil with good. (Romans 12:17–21)

What a brilliant concept. Treat the abrasive people in your life with dignity. Do good to your enemy. Meet their physical needs, and you will suppress evil and thereby make the world a better place.

WAYS TO LOVE YOUR ENEMY

SERVE THEIR FAVORITE MEAL

When you feed your enemy, don't just serve leftovers or tasteless gruel. Deliver deliciousness. That surprise—coming from their enemy—will make those burning coals extra hot and their scalps will burn with curiosity. They will wonder, "What is your motivation?"

MEET THEIR NEEDS AND YOU BECOME THE HERO

The contentious core beliefs of your enemy are likely shaped by a void or brokenness in their life. Help fill that void or heal that brokenness and you will be shining light into a long-standing darkness—a darkness that may have brought your enemy decades of suffering. The Bible instructs, *"Have nothing to do with the fruitless deeds of darkness, but rather expose them. It is shameful even to mention what the disobedient do in secret. But everything exposed by the light becomes visible—and everything that is illuminated becomes a light"* (Ephesians 5:11–13).

SHARE A TABLE

Standing nose to nose with gritted teeth or shouting over ramparts exacerbates any division. Conversely, inviting your enemy to share a meal achieves three strategic goals. One, they are separated from their comrades in malevolence. Two, the neutral setting allows for honest dialogue. Three, both parties are humanized, which breaks down stereotypes and reveals a shared humanity. Actually sitting down over a pizza, plates of nachos, or a charcuterie board flips the script. Sharing food eases tension. (That is, unless you take the last piece of pizza or the cheesiest nacho.)

LITERALLY BREAK BREAD

The term "breaking bread" has spiritual roots as it refers to the Last Supper, which included Jesus laying out the plan of salvation, the introduction of the Holy Spirit, the concept of servant leadership, the prediction of Peter's denial, and the exposure of Judas's betrayal. Introduce your enemy to the union in communion.

☑ CHECKING THE BOX

Hunger is part of the human condition. But much more than physical hunger, every individual has a spiritual hunger that can only be satisfied by knowing Christ. Often, the best way to fight evil is to put down your sword and serve your enemy. That may cause them to rise up in anger or break down in gratitude. Either way, you get their attention.

TO PONDER OR SHARE...

☐ 1. Who are your enemies? Can you imagine inviting them to dinner?

☐ 2. Have you ever wondered why the White House invites despotic, corrupt, or totalitarian dictators to lavish state dinners? Now you know.

☐ 3. How does physical hunger compare to spiritual hunger?

☐ 4. Consider the many food-related lessons and references found in the Bible. That includes the fruit from the Tree of Knowledge of Good and Evil (see Genesis 2:16–17), manna in the desert (see Exodus 16:31–32), dietary laws in the book of Leviticus (see Leviticus 11), Jesus feeding the multitude with five loaves and two fishes (see Matthew 14:19), and the Last Supper (see Matthew 26:17–29).

☐ 5. What does it mean that feeding your enemy will "heap burning coals on his head"? How is that helpful?

25

PROCLAIM SCRIPTURE

*"I never saw a useful Christian who was not a
student of the Bible."*[44]
—D. L. Moody

Google "greatest speeches of all time" and you get an impressive list.

Winston Churchill's stirring 1940 speech, during some of the darkest hours of World War II, pledged, "We shall fight on the beaches...we shall fight in the hills; we shall never surrender."

Hall-of-Famer Lou Gehrig, battling a disabling disease that would eventually take his life just two years later, delivered a touching farewell-to-baseball speech in 1939, calling himself "the luckiest man on the face of the earth."

President Abraham Lincoln, dedicating a national cemetery during the Civil War in his famous 1863 Gettysburg Address, opened his short, approximately 270-word speech with reference to a new nation brought forth just "four score and seven years ago...."

A typical list of inspiring speeches also includes Martin Luther King Jr.'s "I Have a Dream" speech, President John F. Kennedy's

---

44. D. L. Moody, quoted in Josiah Hotchkiss Gilbert, *Dictionary of Burning Words of Brilliant Writers* (1895), 40.

address on the decision to go to the moon, and President Ronald Reagan's remarks at the Brandenburg Gate in Berlin, Germany.

Often overlooked by modern culture are the greatest speeches found in the greatest book of all time.

At the end of his life, Joshua confronts the nation of Israel with a choice. He spends several minutes reminding the people gathered in the valley of Shechem that God has been faithful for generations despite their frequent idolatrous ways. He then challenges the crowds to, *"Choose today whom you will serve,"* finishing with the assertion, *"As for me and my family, we will serve the LORD"* (Joshua 24:15 NLT).

Paul, known as the most influential letter writer of all time, was also quite the orator. One example is Acts chapters 20 to 26, his farewell to the Ephesian elders and his own defense during his trials before the Sanhedrin and other accusers. The passage includes statements like this, *"I consider my life worth nothing to me; my only aim is to finish the race and complete the task the Lord Jesus has given me—the task of testifying to the good news of God's grace"* (Acts 20:24).

Surely the orations of Jesus Himself rank among the greatest ever, including the Sermon on the Mount, the parables in Matthew 13, and his series of teachings on the Mount of Olives foretelling the end times.

What do these examples mean for followers of Christ today? For one thing, if you're called to preach, then gather your notes and prepare to deliver grand sermons with authority. But even if you're not a public speaker, these examples show how you can have tremendous impact with words, spoken quietly and sincerely to those in your own circle of influence.

The good news is that the most powerful words worth speaking have already been written. What's more, they will always have tremendous impact. Quote from the Bible and you are guaranteed to make an impact. You may not see it, and the harvest may take a while, but speaking God's Word will always produce fruit. "*My word. I send it out, and it always produces fruit. It will accomplish all I want it to, and it will prosper everywhere I send it*" (Isaiah 55:11 NLT).

To check the box of proclaiming God's Word, you need to know God's Word. Search your Bible for truths and insights God might be calling you to learn by heart so that you can share with confidence. There are words of wisdom and encouragement for everyone in need. The world is waiting.

GOD'S WORD WORKS

FOR LONELY PEOPLE

"*I will not leave you as orphans; I will come to you*" (John 14:18).

FOR PARENTS

"*Fathers, do not exasperate your children; instead, bring them up in the training and instruction of the Lord*" (Ephesians 6:4).

FOR ANYONE FACING TEMPTATION

"*God is faithful, and he will not let you be tempted beyond your ability, but with the temptation he will also provide the way of escape, that you may be able to endure it*" (1 Corinthians 10:13 ESV).

FOR FRIENDS OR FAMILY MEMBERS FEELING OLD ON THEIR BIRTHDAY

"*I will be your God throughout your lifetime—until your hair is white with age. I made you, and I will care for you. I will carry you along and save you*" (Isaiah 46:4 NLT).

FOR SOMEONE FRUSTRATED AND IMPATIENT

"*Let us not grow weary of doing good, for in due season we will reap, if we do not give up*" (Galatians 6:9 ESV).

FOR ANYONE WEEPING

"*You turned my wailing into dancing; you removed my sackcloth and clothed me with joy*" (Psalm 30:11).

FOR THOSE WHO STRUGGLE WITH THEIR FAITH

"Now faith is confidence in what we hope for and assurance about what we do not see" (Hebrews 11:1).

It's a resource that never fails. Read the Bible as more than just a history book or personal guidebook, actively seeking out verses that could be meaningful to the people you care about. Memorize a few. Then a few more. Speak encouraging words into their lives—not just your words, but God's perfect Word.

☑ CHECKING THE BOX

Proclaiming and sharing God's Word is an act of love. But don't be surprised if giving that gift to others washes back to you with new insight and application for your own life. *"All Scripture is God-breathed and is useful for teaching, rebuking, correcting and training in righteousness, so that the servant of God may be thoroughly equipped for every good work"* (2 Timothy 3:16–17).

TO PONDER OR SHARE...

☐ 1. What historic speeches have inspired you?

☐ 2. Is it enough to "hide God's Word in your heart"? (See Psalm 119:11.)

☐ 3. What verses have proven to be so meaningful to you that you could recite them word for word without the intentional act of memorization?

☐ 4. When is it important to know a verse word for word, and when is it enough to simply understand its core teaching or meaning?

☐ 5. What frequently applicable passages from the Bible can you paraphrase but don't know verbatim? What's keeping you from committing it to memory?

26

DECIDE YOU HAVE ENOUGH

"For after all, the best thing one can do when it is raining, is to let it rain."[45]
—Henry Wadsworth Longfellow

Wouldn't it be nice to have enough of everything you need? Enough food. Enough sleep. Enough closet space. Enough battery life. Enough retirement savings. Enough knowledge to start and finish a project.

Well, maybe you already do. Maybe the idea of "enough" is a choice you can make. Yes, you could always have more. But saying "no" to that third slice of pizza, setting the alarm an hour earlier, cleaning out your closet, powering down your phone, living simpler, and taking the first step on that project are decisions you can make.

Instead of continually scrambling for more, one of the best boxes you can check is "enough." That decision alone will ease you closer to that beautiful concept known as contentment.

The theme of contentment pops up several times in the Bible. Philippians 4:12 comes to mind. *"I know what it is to be in need, and I know what it is to have plenty. I have learned the secret of being*

---

45. Henry Wadsworth Longfellow, "The Poet's Tale: The Birds of Killingworth," in *Tales of a Wayside Inn*, ed. Helen Woodrow Bones (Chicago: A. Flanagan Company, 1913), 142.

content in any and every situation, whether well fed or hungry, whether living in plenty or in want."

How does the idea of choosing contentment sound to you? For some, it sounds heavenly. You are more than ready to stop pursuing more and more and more. For others, settling for mere contentment sounds deadly dull. You might be thinking, "I don't want to be merely satisfied. There's no passion. There's no adrenaline rush. It's boring."

Whether you're leaning toward having enough or craving for more, the *"secret of being content"* described in Philippians 4:12 comes with a surprising punchline. Paul's words—written from prison by the way—may seem like he's talking about slowing down and taking life as it comes, but really that entire passage is about empowerment. The very next verse is inspiring! *"I can do all things through him who gives me strength"* (Philippians 4:13).

Do you get it? When Paul says he has uncovered the secret to being content, he's saying, "I have found the launchpad for doing great things! Once you make the decision that you have enough, you can begin to trust God for His daily provision, and wondrous achievements will follow."

That trust impacts your life and, perhaps, the lives of many people you may never meet.[46]

EMPOWERED BY CONTENTMENT

SETTLING INTO GOD'S PERFECT PROVISION GIVES YOU CONFIDENCE

Suddenly you can put yourself out there. You're trusting Him. You're finally understanding that He cares for you and loves you just the way you are. The pressure is off. You have nothing to prove. You can dream dreams and explore life without panicking about success or failures. He loves you when your cup is empty and when it overflows into the lives of others.

---

46. Adapted from Jay Payleitner, *The Next Verse* (New Kensington, PA: Whitaker House, 2022), 50–53.

DECIDING YOU HAVE ENOUGH MAKES SHARING EASY

Taking inventory of your resources may reveal you have an untapped ability to make the lives of others easier. But you'll only discover this if you enter your self-assessment with a mind open to answering the question, "How much do I really need?"

GRABBING LESS LEAVES MORE FOR OTHERS

It's called gleaning. As described in the book of Ruth, gleaning was God's command to productive farmers to deliberately leave a portion of the harvest behind so that the poor, through their own labor, could gather that grain and provide for themselves.

DECIDING YOU HAVE ENOUGH FREES YOU TO EXPAND YOUR PERSONAL MISSION

A great example of this principle is found in looking at folks who approach retirement with the idea that it's their time to relax and put themselves first. Quite often God reveals other plans. Soon they realize retirement is *not* enough, and they discover untapped resources—time, money, talent—to do great and unexpected work for neighbors, family, and people they may never meet on this side of heaven.

The overarching point is that we can trust God. Have you stopped and thought about the phrase from the Lord's Prayer, *"give us this day our daily bread"*? (See Matthew 6:11.) That may sound like a prayer of request, but really it's an expression of surrendering to the idea that God's provision is always enough. All we really need is *"our daily bread."* He sees the big picture. He knows exactly what we need now and for all eternity.

☑ CHECKING THE BOX

Another way to prove this principle is to ask, "When is enough enough?" A person who doesn't understand the concept that contentment can be found in God's provision will never be satisfied, never be happy, and never find rest. As we confirmed in chapter one, hard work is a healthy strategy and a valuable tool for life. But you can choose to work hard while at the same time understanding, appreciating, and delighting in the fact that you really do have enough.

TO PONDER OR SHARE...

☐ 1. How much is enough? How much more do you need?

☐ 2. What is your motivation for craving more? Is it selfish or honorable?

☐ 3. How can having more than you need be dangerous?

☐ 4. How is deciding you have enough related to trusting God for today and for all eternity?

☐ 5. Do you have a trustworthy financial planner? Do you have a spiritual mentor?

27

EXHIBIT EMPATHY

"You never really understand a person until you consider things from his point of view...until you crawl into his skin and walk around in it."[47]
—Atticus Finch, To Kill a Mockingbird by Harper Lee

Perhaps the most powerful tool we have for impacting the lives of others is empathy.

Please note: There is a difference between empathy and sympathy. In simplest terms, it's all about whether or not you choose to keep an emotional distance. When an acquaintance is hurting, go ahead and put that polite Hallmark sympathy card in the mail. That's a perfectly appropriate and welcome social response. But that expression of sympathy is really just a transaction, not part of a relationship, which requires vulnerability and a personal investment

Empathy, on the other hand, calls for you to come alongside your friends or family members while providing space for them to share their feelings and emotions, even negative ones. Put another way, with sympathy you might "feel *for*" someone, but empathy creates a pathway to "feel *with*" them. Checking that box creates a deeper connection, enabling you to join in their suffering, lighten

---

47. Harper Lee, *To Kill a Mockingbird* (J.B. Lippincott Company, 1960 renewed 1988), 32–33.

their load, and maybe even turn a negative into a positive. As described in 1 Corinthians 12:26, *"If one member suffers, all suffer together; if one member is honored, all rejoice together"* (ESV).

In many ways, heartfelt empathy is proof of love. It's fairly easy to feel sympathy for an unknown stranger or even an enemy, but empathy generates genuine compassion. That's why it's possible for authentic Christians to have empathy for a lost person on the other side of the planet. Our hearts are opened by recognizing God's love for all of humanity and sharing that same worldview.

Earlier in my career I wrote and produced dozens of radio broadcasts that raised funds to provide humanitarian aid, dig wells, send doctors, and print Bibles for underserved people groups around the world. Crafting these broadcasts, our sincere goal was always to spur authentic empathy with listeners. If a donor happened to be motivated by guilt, ego, or self-aggrandizement, the ministry would still accept their money to be distributed for these good works. And surely, God would use it. But I believe financial gifts prompted by sincere empathy had a more lasting impact because that generosity was likely inspired by the Holy Spirit and supported in prayer.

Allowing empathy to open your heart to those near or far may be the most compelling trigger for making the world a better place.

THE IMPACT OF EMPATHY

EMPATHY SOLIDIFIES RELATIONSHIP

People in our lives will never really know we care unless we first listen, feel, and do our best to understand what they're going through.

EMPATHY COMES WITH A BLUEPRINT

Simply match their emotions. When their heart is broken, be heartbroken with them. When they're worried about some challenge or conflict coming up this weekend, be worried with them.

When they're celebrating a victory, celebrate with them. When they're frustrated because something is happening over which they have no control, share their disappointment. Romans 12:15 says it succinctly, *"Rejoice with those who rejoice; mourn with those who mourn."*

EMPATHY BUILDS TRUST

When a relative, colleague, or even stranger realizes you are listening, validating, connecting, and caring, they will feel comfortable revealing even more of their ongoing struggles. How you respond is up to you, but that's information you can use to make their life better.

EMPATHY OPENS THE DOOR TO THE GOSPEL

Jesus becoming man was the ultimate example of empathy. God became flesh in order to show us how to live—even in our fragile human state—and He took on all our temptations and vulnerabilities.

> *For we do not have a high priest who is unable to empathize with our weaknesses, but we have one who has been tempted in every way, just as we are—yet he did not sin.*
>
> (Hebrews 4:15)

No matter what we are going through, Jesus understands. He took on human flesh in order to empathize with our pains, troubles, and sicknesses. In our own way, we can do the same. When we approach people with humility, respect, and compassion, they are more receptive to what we have to say.

☑ CHECKING THE BOX

Consider society's most horrific ills. Authentic Christians know the answers can be found in turning to God and the Bible. That's a message that needs to be heard. Without belaboring the point, delivering that good news is not possible without first demonstrating empathy. Until then, conflict between ethnicities, religions, generations, political parties, labor negotiators, media influencers, gender ideologies, and really any opposing factions will continue to escalate without restraint.

TO PONDER OR SHARE...

☐ 1. Can you differentiate between sympathy, pity, kindness, altruism, and empathy?

☐ 2. Why is empathy important to a preacher, mentor, parent, or even a radio producer working on raising funds for an outreach project?

☐ 3. Specifically, how does empathy open the doors to sharing the gospel?

☐ 4. Should you ever fake empathy? How do you turn an intellectual awareness of someone's emotions into authentic compassion and empathy?

☐ 5. When might you next employ the biblical strategy of Romans 12:15?

28

ACT JUSTLY

"The truth of the matter is that you always know the right thing to do. The hard part is doing it."[48]
—Norman Schwarzkopf

As he was making his final kick in a cross-country race in his home country of Spain, Iván Fernández Anaya had resigned himself to a second-place finish when a surprising opportunity presented itself. The sole runner ahead of him, Olympic medalist Abel Mutai, suddenly stopped running. Fernández Anaya quickly caught up with Mutai and just as quickly realized what was happening. Confused by the signage, the Kenyan thought he had crossed the finish line.

Instead of passing him and claiming victory, the Spaniard stayed just behind Mutai and, using gestures, guided his opponent the final ten meters to the line letting him cross first.

In the months that followed, the media and sports fans both praised and vilified Fernández Anaya for the decision he had made in the moment. He could have won. But would the victory have been earned? Would it have been just?

After the race, the twenty-four-year-old Anaya said, "I did what I had to do. He was the rightful winner. He created a gap

48. Herbert Norman Schwarzkopf Jr., quoted in Linda Picone, *The Daily Book of Positive Quotations* (Minneapolis, MN: 2008), 326.

that I couldn't have closed if he hadn't made a mistake. As soon as I saw he was stopping, I knew I wasn't going to pass him."

In other words—according to the runner who placed second— justice was done. His competitor had earned the right to cross the finish line first. The adage, "May the best man wins," comes to mind. In the quest for justice, the outcome is determined by merit, skill, and worthiness. That mindset motivated Fernández Anaya's split-second decision.

I hope you agree with his conclusion. And I hope we can apply that same principle of justice to our own lives and our relationships with the other inhabitants of this planet.

The checkable box "act justly" may resonate with some readers. It's the first part of a three-part instruction for reconciliation with God found in the Old Testament. I know it well because we have a piece of framed art in our family room featuring that verse, condensed to three bullet points: "Act Justly. Love Mercy. Walk Humbly." In its entirety the verse says, *"What does the* LORD *require of you? To act justly and to love mercy and to walk humbly with your God"* (Micah 6:8).

Although those instructions seem short and sweet, they are infinitely deep. They suggest three critical skills we all need for decision-making. Justice, mercy, humility. Our head, our heart, and our gut.

Like Fernández Anaya, our first instinct should be in terms of what is fair, nondiscriminatory, and just. Second, mercy which, was modeled for us on the cross at Calvary, should anchor our emotions when dealing with any kind of conflict. Third, humility puts God first, puts others next, and surprisingly leads to our own elevated status. *"Humble yourselves before the Lord, and he will exalt you"* (James 4:10 ESV).

The idea of justice has been given a bad rap recently because it gets linked with high-profile cases where the media, the courts, or social influencers drive a subversive narrative and agenda that proves divisive. The result is the opposite of justice. Much of what is labeled "social justice" degenerates into identity politics, unintended consequences, cancel culture, and lack of accountability. The legal process is overruled by intimidation, and bad guys are exalted.

Still, we should all agree that the fair and impartial application of justice is the cornerstone of a healthy society—and, for Christians, something that God Himself has commanded us to pursue. Checking that box makes the world a better place.

IMPLEMENTING JUSTICE

JUSTICE LEVELS THE PLAYING FIELD

Everyone gets treated equally under the law. In the court system and in public opinion, you shouldn't judge or be judged by your bank account, political affiliation, marginalized status, family history, eye color, nationality, age, tattoos, facial hair, or fashion choices.

JUSTICE PROTECTS RIGHTS AND CREATES OPPORTUNITIES

As Martin Luther King Jr. said, individuals should be judged "by the content of their character." When that happens, the best person for any job gets the job, and the person who did the crime does the time.

JUSTICE ULTIMATELY CAN'T COME FROM A GOVERNMENT

Justice may sometimes take a lifetime or more, but God's justice will reign. Proverbs 29:26 maintains, *"Many seek an audience with a ruler, but it is from the LORD that one gets justice."*

JUSTICE PROMOTES HUMAN DIGNITY AND REWARDS INTEGRITY

When criminals walk and laziness gets rewarded, that dishonors and mocks anyone who does an honest day's work.

When justice reigns, the inherent worth and dignity of every individual—no matter their age, skin tone, disability, height, weight, wardrobe choices, body odor, personality quirks, or anything else—is acknowledged and respected. Doing the right thing requires all of us to take steps to ensure hard work is rewarded, equality is intrinsic to our interactions, and the individual who runs fastest gets the first-place trophy.

☑ CHECKING THE BOX

Whatever happened to people knowing "the right thing to do"? Despite cultural differences, personal biases, varying levels of intelligence, and other situational complexities, past generations were not stumped by that concept. At one time, you could count on people to return a lost wallet, treat dogs humanely, pick up their picnic trash, not cheat at Monopoly, and respectfully wait their turn at deli counters. At one time, a cross-country runner honoring another runner would not even be questioned. Getting back to those ideals, I'm fairly sure, would make the world a better place.

TO PONDER OR SHARE...

☐ 1. Without any guilt, would you overtake and snatch victory from a lost and confused runner in front of you? (After all, you wouldn't be breaking any rules!)

☐ 2. Why is it difficult to act justly? What holds greater sway in your response: internal factors or eternal pressures?

☐ 3. How has the long-standing idea of justice been impacted by the emergence of social justice?

☐ 4. What happens to a culture in which criminals walk, honesty gets mocked, violence wins, human rights are violated, and laziness gets rewarded?

☐ 5. Taking a closer look at Micah 6:8, what does the Lord require of us?

29

BRIGHTEN THE ROOM

"I'm going to keep having fun every day I have left. Because there's no other way to play it....You just have to decide if you're a Tigger or an Eeyore."[49]
—Randy Pausch

There's a lighthearted yet accurate axiom that goes like this: "Everyone has the ability to brighten a room—some when they enter, others when they exit."

Which kind of person are you?

Truth be told, there's a third category of person that most of us fall into, and that's somewhere in the middle. We're in the room, but our presence neither brightens the room nor dims the lights. We're not Princess Diana, but we're also not Debbie Downer. We're not a party animal or social butterfly, but we're also not a buzzkill or a wet blanket.

In our quest to make the world a better place, does this idea really matter? I think it does. As people see us coming or going, they're going to form an opinion about us. And our objective— both immediately and in the long run—should be to earn the right to make an impact in their lives for the kingdom of God. Which

49. Randy Pausch, "Randy Pausch's Last Lecture: Really Achieving Your Childhood Dreams" (lecture, Carnegie Mellon University, Pittsburgh, PA, September 18), 19, https://www.cs.cmu.edu/~pausch/Randy/pauschlastlecturetranscript.pdf.

means we need to be seen as enjoyable company, not someone who makes everyone in the room remember they have someplace else to be.

Someone once said, "We need to be winsome, it we want to win some for Christ."

But lest we get off track, let's agree on some ground rules for this goal of "brightening a room." It does not require physical beauty, intelligence, fame, fortune, or comic timing. Also, don't approach this assignment as "being the life of the party." Really, you're simply being a gracious and affable presence. This concept applies to any social, business, small group, meet and greet, rally, reunion, fundraiser, grand opening, picnic, housewarming, celebration, or anytime people gather—from three to three thousand.

Here's the challenge—when you "enter a room," consider these options: Stand straight, survey the room, and smile. Be humbly confident. Don't skulk. Ask open-ended questions. Practice active listening. Don't dominate any discussion, but do share short anecdotes that relate to the conversation. Give an occasional sincere compliment. Offer to help the host. And that person standing alone? Include them in the conversation. Be a connector. Use people's names. Mingle. And so on. Really, these are all things your grandma would tell you.

The film *Planes, Trains and Automobiles* features a memorable scene that may be instructive, with Steve Martin as Neal Page and John Candy as Del Griffith. After a frustrating day, Neal realizes he may not make it home for Thanksgiving. Moreover, he finds himself having to spend the night with his unexpected and overbearing traveling companion. In their unkempt motel room, Neal loses his cool with Del and launches into a tirade: "Everything is not an anecdote. You have to discriminate. You choose things that are funny or mildly amusing or interesting. You're a miracle! Your stories have none of that. They're not even amusing accidentally!

By the way, you know, when you're telling these little stories, here's a good idea. Have a point. It makes it so much more interesting for the listener."

Actually, the entire scene is a bit unsettling. But the point is made. Colossians 4:6 says it much kinder and gentler: *"Let your conversation be always full of grace, seasoned with salt, so that you may know how to answer everyone."*

TENETS OF BRIGHTENING A ROOM

While this idea of illuminating a room may not seem of earth-shattering importance, it actually may be the cornerstone to the mission of being a humble and persuasive advocate for a brighter world. It's a box you can check. A box you must check.

YOU ARE NOT THE LIGHT

Lest you think this is all about you, remember that your job is simply to crack open the door, allowing the true Light to flood the room. *"I am the light of the world. Whoever follows me will never walk in darkness, but will have the light of life"* (John 8:12).

BE AN AMBASSADOR

Since our home is in heaven, we enter every room as a representative of another world, carrying a message of love, mercy, and purpose. *"We are therefore Christ's ambassadors, as though God were making his appeal through us. We implore you on Christ's behalf: Be reconciled to God"* (2 Corinthians 5:20).

FIRST DO NO HARM

This fundamental tenet, recognized in medical ethics as part of the Hippocratic Oath, has application to believers who find themselves amidst the general population. If you're conspicuous about being a Christian (see chapter thirty-three) but bring fear, judgment, rudeness, drama, or any kind of negativity when you walk into a room, you've done damage to the kingdom.

LEAVE YOUR CAMPSITE BETTER THAN YOU FOUND IT

This principle, popular with scouting programs, has application for checking this box. When you leave a room, you want to leave a trail of smiles, good tidings, and new friends. The goal is for people to think, "What a swell person," or, "I want what they've got."

Considering the plight of the world, it's understandable why many people focus on the darkness, seeing only murky tunnels without any light at the end. In response, remember this prayer Paul prayed for the church at Ephesus, which recalibrates our focus from this world to our home in eternity: "*I pray that the eyes of your heart may be enlightened in order that you may know the hope to which he has called you, the riches of his glorious inheritance in his holy people*" (Ephesians 1:18).

☑ CHECKING THE BOX

The most obvious way to brighten a room is to exemplify the fruit of the Spirit as described in Galatians 5:22–23 — that is, to showcase "*love, joy, peace, forbearance, kindness, goodness, faithfulness, gentleness and self-control.*"

TO PONDER OR SHARE...

☐ 1. Honestly, what do people currently experience when you walk into a room? Are you a Tigger or an Eeyore? Do you reflect or diminish the light of Christ?

☐ 2. Is your conversational style full of grace and seasoned with salt? Are you an ambassador for Christ?

☐ 3. When chitchat turns to ridiculing and bashing individuals and institutions, what are some ways to inject hope into the conversation?

☐ 4. When have you damaged the kingdom with your words?

☐ 5. Which fruit of the Spirit is your go-to gift? Which might you need to further develop?

30

DEFY THE LIONS

"I [believe] those witnesses that get their throats cut."[50]
—Blaise Pascal

In the first century, Emperor Nero apparently took pleasure in decreeing followers of the early church be sent into the Roman Colosseum to be torn apart by wild animals. The practice was called *damnatio ad bestias* meaning "condemnation to beasts."

More than a method of execution, these "games" became a form of entertainment for centuries, during which some 400,000 people were executed. Carnivorous beasts procured and released into the arena included lions, tigers, leopards, jaguars, and even rhinos and crocodiles.[51]

While the practice of "throwing Christians to the lions" did mostly come to an end after four centuries, the persecution of believers did not. According to Breakpoint.org from the Colson Center, "more Christians died for their faith in the 20th century than the previous 19 combined, and the 21st century is shaping up to be at least as deadly, but likely more."[52]

50. Blaise Pascal quoted in Timothy Keller, *The Reason for God: Belief in an Age of Skepticism* (New York: Riverhead Books, 2008), 218.
51. Fanny, "Damnatio ad Bestias: All About Roman Executions at the Colosseum," Visit Colosseum Rome, https://visit-colosseum-rome.com/damnatio-ad-bestias/.
52. John Stonestreet and Shane Morris, "Updating Foxe: The New Book of Christian Martyrs," Breakpoint, July 24, 2023, https://www.breakpoint.org/updating-foxe-the-new-book-of-christian-martyrs/.

In their well-documented book, *Jesus Freaks, Revolutionaries*, Michael Tait, TobyMac, and Kevin Max (a.k.a. dc Talk) reported that, at the time of their writing in the early 2000s, 69 million Christian have been martyred since Jesus walked the earth.

Forbes magazine published reports that 309 million Christians live in countries where they might suffer very high or extreme levels of persecution and every day, on average, thirteen Christians are killed for their faith.[53]

Do these overwhelming numbers frighten you? Sadden you? Or, hopefully, motivate you to ask how you should respond?

History reveals the real-life example of those willing to make the ultimate sacrifice has been a powerful catalyst in drawing seekers and skeptics into relationship with Christ. The irony is that Nero's goal to entertain the crowds, and deter the new spiritual movement, backfired. As Tertullian, an early church theologian, said, "The blood of the martyrs is the seed of the church."

Still, most of us should not expect to suffer persecution. Or should we? Maybe "checking the boxes" to "make the world a better place" should invite persecution. Maybe speaking up for your beliefs should involve a level of risk.

What actions could you take that might be "the seed of the church"? Perhaps it's standing up for a moral principle on the job. Or quietly being the one employee who doesn't take home office supplies or take credit for someone else's work. It could be challenging a friend to clean up his language and stop taking the Lord's name in vain. Or joining a pro-life rally, visiting prisons, or praying in public. What if you secured a seat on the city council or school board and thoughtfully began quoting scripture? What if you actively began sharing the gospel with your hostile neighbor?

53. Ewelina U. Ochab, "One In Eight Christians Worldwide Live In Countries Where They May Face Persecution," *Forbes*, January 13, 2021, https://www.forbes.com/sites/ewelinaochab/2021/01/13/one-in-eight-christians-worldwide-live-in-countries-where-they-would-be-persecuted/?sh=6b7e8a3f5016.

Would such actions lead to physical persecution? Probably not. But it could take you out of your comfort zone. And that's a pretty good start.

SUMMARIZING EARLY CHRISTIAN MARTYRDOM

WHO ARE THE REAL LIONS

In first-century Rome, remember it wasn't the beasts who were the bad guys—it was those in power who felt confused, scared, and threatened by this new sect. Let's give the actual carnivores credit! They helped showcase the dedication of the earliest Christians.

WHO WOULD DIE FOR A LIE

We can trust the testimony of the eleven apostles who chose martyrdom rather than deny the reality of Jesus's identity as the Messiah and Son of God. They knew the real Jesus. They met the resurrected Christ. If Jesus wasn't legit, those men would have scattered, the New Testament would not have been written, and the Christian faith would have fizzled out soon after the tomb was sealed.

REMEMBER STEPHEN

He was the first martyr. False testimony led to his arrest. As recorded in Acts chapter seven, his stirring response to the charges turned the tables on the Jewish high priest and other religious leaders, incriminating them of failing to obey God's laws for generations and of killing Jesus. Gnashing their teeth in anger, they stoned Stephen and laid their cloaks at the feet of a young man named Saul. Stephen's death serves as a pivotal connecting point between the Old Law and the New Law. The day of his murder, the focus of reaching others for Christ changed from local to global.

MEET JUSTIN MARTYR

Justin was a respected second-century pagan philosopher who bounced from philosophy to philosophy, looking for answers.

Eventually he met an old man, a Christian, who faithfully shared the gospel—and Justin converted! Justin's newfound faith was bolstered as he reflected on the lives of martyrs, realizing the credibility of a faith that had caused so many men and women to sacrifice their lives for it. Eventually, Justin went on to be a martyr himself, but not before writing these powerful words: "Though beheaded, and crucified, and thrown to wild beasts, and chains, and fire, and all other kinds of torture, we do not give up our confession; but the more such things happen, the more do others and in larger numbers become faithful, and worshippers of God through the name of Jesus."[54]

We already know how the world will respond to our message. The almost certain rejection comes in many forms: mockery, ridicule, indifference, contempt, or even persecution. Those who don't know Jesus don't want to hear the truth. They don't want to be told right from wrong. Their eyes are blinded, and they prefer it that way. Jesus himself confirms the social status of every authentic believer: *"You do not belong to the world, but I have chosen you out of the world. That is why the world hates you"* (John 15:19).

☑ CHECKING THE BOX

> Second Timothy 3:12 tells us, *"Everyone who wants to live a godly life in Christ Jesus will be persecuted."* Maybe we need to be asking ourselves, "What actions might I undertake that would give glory to God, even though I could be persecuted for my beliefs?"

TO PONDER OR SHARE...

☐ 1. Does the pervasiveness of persecution against Christians in today's world surprise you?

☐ 2. What does it mean to "belong to the world"? Do you feel as if you have been "chosen out of this world"?

54. St. Justin Martyr, "Dialogue with Trypho," Early Christian Writings, chapter CX, https://www.earlychristianwritings.com/text/justinmartyr-dialoguetrypho.html.

☐   3.   While Stephen was being stoned (see Acts 7:54–60), a young Pharisee named Saul watched the coats of the attackers, approved of the stoning, and then began his own reign of terror over Christianity. Do you know what later happened to Saul? (See Acts 9:1–19.)

☐   4.   Can persecution have a silver lining? Furthermore, can God use all things—including evil—for good? (See Romans 8:28.)

☐   5.   Have you ever been mocked, scorned, bullied, ostracized, or harassed for your authentic faith? Congratulations!

31

INSPIRE CHILDREN TO SOAR

"Every child you encounter is a divine appointment. With each one you have the power and opportunity to build the child up or tear the child down."[55]
—Wess Stafford, former CEO of Compassion International

This chapter is not just for parents. How children are welcomed and treated in this world—by anybody and everybody—may have a greater impact on the future of our world than just about any other factor.

Here's the concern: Many people expect the worst from children. Kids—from delivery to independence—are seen as an inconvenience, an expense, and destined for trouble. Frankly, that can be true! Especially because people who perceive children as a burden are paving the way for a self-fulling prophecy.

By treating children as if they are a burden, their lives—and yours—become tragedies waiting to happen. Abort a child, and the hole in your heart lasts forever. Neglect to snuggle, smile, and whisper words of love with your newborn, and you stifle that little one's ability to give love or feel love. School-aged children are not as resilient as you may think. Heaping shame, hostility, and ridicule

---

55. Wess Stafford, *Too Small to Ignore: Why the Least of These Matters Most* (New York: WaterBrook, 2007), 9.

on a teenager begets a young adult who feels worthless, rebels, and expects a future devoid of purpose or hope.

The opposite is also true. With thoughtful and loving adults in their lives, children have a chance to thrive. They are far less likely to become a burden on families, communities, and the world.

Psalm 127:3–5 establishes the foundation for that preferable outcome: "*Children are a gift from the* LORD; *they are a reward from him. Children born to a young man are like arrows in a warrior's hands. How joyful is the man whose quiver is full of them*" (NLT).

Accepting the children in your life as gifts opens the door for them to become a reward, a dividend, a blessing. They bring fulfillment to life, so much so that having lots of kids—a full quiver—is a source of joy.

The image of children as "*arrows in a warrior's hands*" places parents and caregivers in the roles of "steadfast archers." Even if you've never held a bow and arrow, envision yourself as empowered, strong, and confident. You reach over your shoulder and extract a single arrow from your quiver. You have crafted that arrow with care, making sure the shaft is straight and true, the arrowhead sharp, and the feathered fletching precise. As a disciplined archer, it feels natural to slide the notch of the arrow onto the bowstring. Combining strength and gentleness, you pull that arrow toward you, close to your heart. Because you've invested the time, you know the gift and talents of each child, earning you the right to help choose a target that's exactly right for this exact arrow. You remain steadfast, feet planted firm. With a slight smile, you let the beloved arrow fly. Then, you do it again. And again. With each one of your kids. Until your quiver is empty. Just as God planned.

In a surprising twist, there's significant personal reward in checking this box. As the children in your life soar to rewarding destinations, you find satisfaction in who they are and what they achieve. In many ways, it's all about them. But feel free to take a bit of credit for everything they do to make the world a better place.

STEPS TO RELEASING A CHILD'S POTENTIAL

SET YOUR OWN FEET ON SOLID ROCK

The adults in a child's life become the foundation from which they can launch themselves into the world. Your steadfastness gives them courage to head off to kindergarten, summer camp, auditions and tryouts, the military, college, and the workplace. They know, if they need you, you'll be there.

EXPECT A BATTLE FOR YOUR CHILDREN'S HEARTS AND MINDS

Enter their world with regular intentionality so you can understand how Satan targets our young people. Early on, spearhead the fight. Later, stand side-by-side. The goal is to equip them to do battle on their own.

POLISHED ARROWS ARE READY TO FLY

Raised with unconditional love and with a track record of commitment and determination, children will advance into the world with confidence—not whining, making excuses, trapped in selfish indulgence, or paralyzed by a spirit of fear.

EVERY CHILD HAS THE POTENTIAL TO SOAR

Of course, every child is different—even siblings. Each comes with their own gifts, challenges, imagination, fears, resilience, learning styles, attention span, sleep patterns, and so much more. Still, let's give every child a chance to embrace hope, know the Creator, and recognize their true value. To their family. To the world. To God.

THEIR TARGET TRANSCENDS THEIR OWN AGENDA

Adults need to see young people—and themselves—as part of the solution to the divisiveness and crud of this world.

Let's all pledge to see the potential in every child we meet, but also to recognize them as unfinished works in progress. Soon enough they will put aside their childlike innocence and ignorance. *"When I was a child, I talked like a child, I thought like a child, I reasoned like a child. When I became a man, I put the ways of childhood behind me"* (1 Corinthians 13:11).

☑ CHECKING THE BOX

Instead of being exasperated by children, let's see them as God sees them: treasured people, made in His image, whom we are blessed to protect, provide for, and help prepare for the future. Right now, they can't possibly know everything. Honestly, they are supposed to mess up and push the limits! But that doesn't mean they're a burden. By nurturing them with unconditional love and instilling winsome expectations in them for their future, we help prepare them to do great things. Children are a gift to be opened—and then set free to explore.

TO PONDER OR SHARE...

☐ 1. What young people are in your life? (There may be more than you realize.)

☐ 2. What is the purpose of childhood?

☐ 3. With all the time, money, and effort it takes to raise a child, how can they possibly be a "reward"?

☐ 4. When children of any age are hurting, how can we come alongside their parents with love and empathy, rather than judgment and avoidance?

☐ 5. As a steadfast archer assigned to launch children into the world, are your own feet set on solid rock?

32

CHILL OUT

*"How much more grievous are the consequences of anger
than the causes of it."*
—Marcus Aurelius

Is the world getting angrier? I think so. That may even be one of my primary motivations for writing this book. Keeping our collective temper could go a long way toward making the world a better place. It turns out most of the world-changing boxes within these chapters are impossible to check while you're angry.

Not long ago, reasonable people who disagreed mostly kept their cool while engaging in a civil exchange of ideas. Neighbors settled disputes over a cold beverage on a patio. Union contracts and party platforms were hammered out in smoke-filled rooms that may have included heated debate but rarely crossed the line into raging anger. Schoolyard scuffles were resolved with little bloodshed and minimal adult intervention.

Today, anger is the norm. When experts and world leaders gather to take on the many challenges facing the planet, the result is not consensus, but outrage.

Life will always have frustrations and grievances, but emotions escalating to anger is what leads to slammed doors, mass shootings, child abuse, bitter divorce, social isolation, gridlocked negotiations, and even substance abuse and medical challenges—all of which leads to even more outrage and bitterness. Let's all agree that anger triggers more anger and a downward spiral of regret.

How about you? Do you fly into an occasional rage that feels productive and satisfying in the moment, only to realize later that you made a fool of yourself and made the situation worse? Join the club.

Still, because you know your Bible, maybe you justify your actions. You argue that anger itself is morally neutral or even desirable, citing the example of Jesus who displayed anger when He overturned the tables of the moneychangers in the temple. (See Mark 11:15–17.)

That argument misses the point. First, you're not Jesus. Second, we really should distinguish between righteous anger and self-centered anger. Jesus was motivated not by lost car keys or a broken fingernail—but by the desecration of the temple. Quoting the words of the prophet Isaiah, He conveyed a resolute message, stating, *"Is it not written: 'My house will be called a house of prayer for all nations?' But you have made it a 'den of robbers'"* (Mark 11:17).

Third, Jesus knew the repercussions of his actions and was willing to bear the consequences. The very next verse describes how the chief priests, *"began looking for a way to kill him"* (Mark 11:18). When you lose your cool, are you willing to accept the consequences?

It's true that righteous anger, coupled with controlled determination, serves as a fitting response to grave injustices like child abuse, racism, abortion, and similar wrongs. On the contrary, self-centered anger often spirals out of control. Unrestrained, selfish anger ushers you down an undesirable path. Psalm 37:8 advises, *"Refrain from anger, and forsake wrath! Fret not yourself; it tends only to evil"* (esv).

The most compelling rationale for being slow to anger is that it affords you the time to consider the problem you're facing from God's perspective. Perhaps the situation or event triggering your anger is a fragment of God's grander design for your life, an opportunity yet to be unveiled. We get angry when our mortgage application is rejected, yet it could be that God is safeguarding us from purchasing a house on a floodplain. Your daughter doesn't get into her dream school, but at her second-choice college she finds the perfect career, lifelong friends, and a worthy husband. Missing out on a promotion might trigger anger, but that new position would have meant more stress and more time away from the family. These are all aspects known to God, but beyond our grasp.

Consider the parable of the man stranded on a desert island. Even as he imagines things couldn't get any worse, his bamboo hut is obliterated by a bolt of lightning. He shakes his fist at God, yet an hour later, a passing ship rescues him. The captain remarks, "We spotted your smoke signals."

BENEFITS TO MASTERING ANGER

ANGER RARELY MAKES THINGS BETTER

Often anger prevents you from seeing an easy solution to the problem or trusting that God has better things right around the next corner.

KEEPING YOUR COOL PROTECTS RELATIONSHIPS

Proverbs 15:18 confirms, "*A hot-tempered person stirs up conflict, but the one who is patient calms a quarrel.*"

DON'T BE ANGRY AT "THE MEDIA"

Technology, film, books, art, social media, music, and even news outlets are not themselves inherently good or evil. The important thing is how they are used. Faced with morally corrupt use of media, the best Christian response might be to promote, deliver, and support God-honoring alternatives.

CALMLY APPROACHING A CONFLICT MITIGATES HOSTILITY

If you're chill, your adversary might also stay chill. De-escalation brings resolution.

EXPRESSING ONLY RIGHTEOUS ANGER EARNS CREDIBILITY

As stated above, some issues deserve an angry response. But if you're constantly flying off the handle, no one will listen to your next rant, even if it's justified.

Explosive indignation in the face of exasperating circumstances may seem justifiable, but really it signifies our reluctance to accept and follow God's plan. Anger may be a natural human sentiment. However, sooner or later, you will need to decide whether you're willing to embrace the notion that God's far-reaching, infinite perspective deserves your trust.

☑ CHECKING THE BOX

Anger hampers communication. Anger leads to impulsive and irrational decisions. Anger blinds you to any truth that may be spoken by your adversary. Anger enrages enemies and puts yourself and those you care about at risk. When faced with obvious frustration or disappointment, your ability to remain composed causes everyone in your circle of influence to wonder, "Where does that serenity come from?" When they ask, have your answer ready.

TO PONDER OR SHARE...

☐ 1. Is the world getting angrier?

☐ 2. What makes you angry? How do you respond?

☐ 3. Have you ever heard or used the excuse, "Well Jesus got angry, so it must be okay"?

☐ 4. When anger is righteous and therefore justified, does that give you permission to lose your cool?

☐ 5. What are some possible benefits (and drawbacks) of explosive anger?

33

BE CONSPICUOUS

"A holy life will produce the deepest impression. Lighthouses blow no horns; they only shine."[56]
—D. L. Moody

If you were put on trial for being a Christian, would there be enough evidence to convict you?

I'm not sure who first asked that question, but a person's answer to it is a pretty solid gauge for whether or not their approach to life is making the world a better place. If you're convinced the world is lost without Jesus, then it seems you should be living in such a way that people notice your faith and how it impacts your life.

Please note, this short chapter will not implore you to live in perfect righteousness. That's impossible. Also "being conspicuous" doesn't mean painting "I'm a Christian" on your garage door or hiring a truck with giant speakers to travel your neighborhood blaring that kind of message. Rather, the way to check that box is to live a life that reflects Christian principles—many of which are reflected in this book—and then humbly let people know that your joy and purpose has a source. A few examples might be in order.

Pray at restaurants. Before you recoil in horror, let me explain how that might look. Whether your dinner party is just two people

---

56. "The Quotable Moody," D. L. Moody Center, accessed March 18, 2024, https://moodycenter.org/the-quotable-moody-d-l-moody-quotes/.

or twenty, grasp hands around the table, enlist one person to quietly speak less than twenty words, and don't draw attention to yourself. What's the point? Primarily, you're thanking God for the food and company. But more than that, a few people may notice and think, "Huh, I guess faith is alive and well in some families."

Of course, for the rest of the meal, your dining partners need to refrain from throwing food across the room, loudly complaining about the overcooked pork chops, acting rude toward the waitress, or any other mayhem. Plus, you should probably tip well and not squeal your tires leaving the parking lot. But if muted laughter and good conversation flow from your table to the rest of the restaurant, that's a victory. You've modeled faith as a virtue.

Similarly, most of the families in your neighborhood should know that you identify as a follower of Christ. Your regular smiles, occasional thoughtful gestures, and unpretentious mention of answered prayers and meaningful passages of Scripture should add up to a conspicuous faith. At the same time, you really can't let your dandelions spread to your neighbor's lawn, play basketball in your driveway past 10:00 p.m., or curse your dog when he runs out the front door with your slipper in his mouth.

On the job, colleagues who see you reading your Bible at lunch must not also see you stealing office supplies, fudging expense reports, or trashing the restroom. Rather, be the kind of employee or boss that shows up on time, gives credit to other team members, respects diversity, and welcomes new hires. Don't be surprised when your conspicuous faith lures a coworker to your workstation when they have a personal crisis or need some prayer. That's what Jesus was talking about when He called Peter and friends to be "fishers of men." (See Matthew 4:19.)

People passing through your life should see evidence that you put God first and of how your faith brings light to a dark world. As Jesus said in the Sermon on the Mount:

"You are the light of the world. A town built on a hill cannot be hidden. Neither do people light a lamp and put it under a bowl. Instead they put it on its stand, and it gives light to everyone in the house. In the same way, let your light shine before others, that they may see your good deeds and glorify your Father in heaven." (Matthew 5:14–16)

An initial reading of this passage might lead a person to think this passage is all about them: *"You are the light...let your light shine...your good deeds."* It's true that your faith should be visible and attractive, but the last phrase clarifies why you were given that light in the first place: It's all about God, so that you can *"glorify your Father in heaven."*

SHINING YOUR LIGHT FOR CHRIST

Don't hide your faith. Don't make excuses or apologize for being a follower of Christ. Instead, be a role model, mentor, and humble servant. Enticing even one person to turn to the light of Christ makes the world a better place.

KNOW YOU ARE BEING WATCHED

The world loves to point out vulnerabilities and weak spots in the armor of God's people. Take that as a challenge to be your best self and live with integrity. When you mess up—and you will—do what it takes to make things right.

BE A LIGHTHOUSE

When a friend, family member, or colleague is facing the storms of life, you have the truth and love that can be a beacon guiding lost souls home. Stand tall. Shine bright. Give hope.

BE WINSOME, NOT BRASH

Shy away from the garish worldly entanglements that shine deceptively bright. Like flashing neon, they get attention, but those deceptive destructive lights might best be described as human bug zappers.

DON'T SEEK SELF-SERVING ATTENTION

Being conspicuous with your faith is not about saying, "Look at me." Being too conspicuous is clearly warned against in the Sermon on the Mount. Jesus said, *"Be careful not to practice your righteousness in front of others to be seen by them. If you do, you will have no reward from your Father in heaven"* (Matthew 6:1).

It's a bit of a balancing act. To outsiders, a Christian should look like they have their act together. You celebrate when good stuff happens. You roll with the punches and keep smiling when not-so-good things happen. But you never forget the source of your confidence and security. The goal is to live a life that's desirable, even enviable, all while knowing in your heart *"the joy of the LORD is your strength"* (Nehemiah 8:10).

☑ CHECKING THE BOX

Here's an idea. Think about a dozen acquaintances from different areas of life including neighbors, home repairmen, postal workers, baristas, coworkers, suppliers, and people you see regularly at the gym, community gatherings, school, and other places around town. Do they know you call yourself a Christian? Would they be surprised?

TO PONDER OR SHARE...

☐ 1. Do you hide your faith? Or do you let your light shine?

☐ 2. Should you have an ichthus fish on your bumper? What are the risks?

☐ 3. How long does it take when meeting someone new before they know you are a follower of Christ?

☐ 4. What are some ways new friends or coworkers can discern you're a Christian without your explicitly stating it?

☐ 5. Have you ever had a casual acquaintance come to you for advice, prayer, or emotional support because they knew you were a person of faith?

34

GIVE WORTHWHILE FEEDBACK

"Feedback is the breakfast of champions."[57]
—Rick Tate

If someone trusts you enough to ask your opinion, you should be honored, you should be honest, and you should be careful not to squash their creativity or pull the plug on their ambition.

When a project manager, event planner, producer, artist, author, athlete, or other professional asks your opinion, then it's imperative that you give them genuine, thoughtful, and worthwhile feedback. Insight they can use. But also, don't overwhelm them with ideas that belittle, burden, discourage, or shut down the entire project.

Families are excellent testing grounds for giving opinions. The most obvious example is the classic question from a wife to her husband: "Does this dress make me look fat?" In that scenario, sharing any assessment is pretty much a no-win situation. But in most other cases, a sincere request for feedback from a family member is a chance to open the doors of communication, share your wisdom and experience, and help them up their game.

---

57. Ken Blanchard, "Feedback is the Breakfast of Champions," August 17, 2009, https://www.kenblanchardbooks.com/feedback-is-the-breakfast-of-champions/

Parents of precocious youngsters can probably relate. For example, how should you respond when a four-year-old presents you with a drawing of what looks like a porcupine playing piano and eating pizza on the porch, and asks, "Do you like it?" You have two choices: (A) crush their little creative spirit, or (B) launch them into a world of stimulating curiosity, expanding possibilities, and thinking slightly or significantly outside the box.

Going out on a limb, I'm going to make this decision for you: Choose B. Here's how that conversation should play out.

Your first response to their fantastical drawing should be obvious. You "oooh" and "aaah." After that, you need to be a little more calculated with your response. Your next goal is to find out what is *actually* in the drawing without letting them know you don't know. So don't say, "What is it?" Instead, invite the little artist up on your lap and say, "Whoa. This is most excellent. Tell me about it." Then start picking up on their verbal cues. Let them point to the indiscernible kayak, Ferris wheel, marching band, or wildebeest. Ask open-ended questions that get them thinking and explaining. "How did you choose these two colors?" "These lines are straight and these are curvy. Why did you choose that?" Partner with them in the discovery of their own creative abilities, and help them see how they have control over the creative choices they make. Point out elements of their artwork that are bold and decisive, even suggesting their efforts have led you to think new thoughts. Let them know that—like all the great works of art—their masterpiece has given you a new perspective on life, the world, or some other grand concept.

After the creative brainstorming session, there's one more critical element of this conversation: You need to bring it to a satisfying closure. One that confirms that you see value in both their effort and their result. Ask, "Can I keep it?" Then ceremoniously slide the artwork into a file folder you have with their name on it. In a rare instance you'll want to have an exceptional piece of art professionally mounted and framed. But for most two-dimensional projects, the file folder is your best answer. You can pull it out anytime—even decades from now—to appreciate this season in their life (even if they don't go on to become a world-famous artist).[58]

If you're a parent of a preschooler, feel free to reenact this scenario in your home in the very near future. That's a worthwhile takeaway from this chapter. But for most readers, the objective is to apply these same principles to offer constructive feedback to older children, friends, colleagues, staff, and anyone who seeks your opinion.

Without belaboring the point, productive feedback should inspire confidence that the project is worth pursuing and the individual seeking input has what it takes to elevate the project to the next level. In general, you don't want to be the person who extinguishes someone else's dream. Whether that dream is to write a Broadway show, go into space, play in the major leagues, open a restaurant, or cure cancer.

If you do have worthwhile input to offer, you can't go wrong with the classic business approach known as the "compliment sandwich." Start with praise, honestly sneak in a bit of constructive criticism, and then end with a word of encouragement.

CONSTRUCTIVE FEEDBACK UPLIFTS AND INSPIRES

Checking this box may not directly make the world better, but your thoughtful feedback might equip someone else to cultivate a brighter future for their own corner of the world.

BEING A CRITIC IS DIFFERENT THAN CRITICIZING

Why do we think we need to point out the flaws in someone's work? Is it to make ourselves feel superior? To show how smart we

---

58. Adapted from Jay Payleitner, *52 Things Kids Need from a Dad* (Eugene, OR: Harvest House Publishers, 2010), 25–26.

are? It's better to see the potential and point out the unpolished gem in their plans.

IMAGINE THE END USER

If you're not the target audience for a project or publication, then it's not helpful to say, "I don't get it," or "That's not my style." It's better to dig into how, when, and why the work will be appreciated by the intended end user.

WATCH YOUR WORDS

When giving feedback, think twice before delivering those first snipes that come to mind: "Doesn't make sense." "That'll never work." "We already tried that." Or, "It seems to me like you're spending a lot of time on this that could be used more productively."

DON'T SUGARCOAT

Helpful feedback provides honest criticism and beneficial suggestions within a framework of encouragement. False praise and meaningless flattery don't help anyone.

TURN YOUR CRITIQUE INTO A CONVERSATION

Ask helpful questions. Don't make snap judgements. Tease out fresh opportunities. Give yourself time to understand the goals and dreams that led to this project. Help them talk out their vision.

It's true that we learn more from our mistakes than our successes. Trial and error is a valid path to improvement. But good feedback accelerates the learning process. Armed with your sensitive and balanced insight, you may help a colleague or entrepreneur avoid a few oversights or fumbles. You can help others do their best work simply by being the kind of person people seek out for advice.

☑ CHECKING THE BOX

As you might expect, the book of Proverbs has much to say about sharing wisdom and giving feedback. *"Listen to advice and accept discipline, and at the end you will be counted among the wise"* (Proverbs 19:20). *"The way of fools seems right to them, but the wise listen to advice"* (Proverbs 12:15). *"Whoever loves discipline loves knowledge, but whoever hates correction is stupid"* (Proverbs 12:1).

TO PONDER OR SHARE...

☐ 1. If someone is not a verified expert, is their insight and feedback worth hearing?

☐ 2. Should you ever offer unsolicited advice and opinions?

☐ 3. Is it more difficult to give feedback to a friend, spouse, employee, third grader, or teenager?

☐ 4. When giving criticism, should you start with the positives or negatives?

☐ 5. Are you more likely to give feedback that derails a project or gets a project back on track?

35

BE A TALENT SCOUT

"Our chief want in life is somebody who shall make us do what we can."[59]
—Ralph Waldo Emerson

Considering the global population of eight billion people, it may seem silly to suggest you have the ability to change the world one person at a time. But don't let that deter you from noticing the potential in someone in your life and giving them a solid dose of encouragement. Maybe even becoming their mentor.

Visionaries and trailblazers who have shaped our world often point out how they were inspired through deliberate one-on-one interactions with a heroic figure. Could you possibly be that kind of hero?

- Sally Ride, the first American woman in space, credited her graduate school physics professor, Dr. Arthur Walker, with encouraging her to apply to NASA's astronaut corps.[60]

- In the 5th century BCE, the Greek philosopher Socrates mentored Plato, who would greatly influence Western

59. Ralph Waldo Emerson, *The Prose Works of Ralph Waldo Emerson: Representative Men. English Traits. Conduct of Life,"* (Boston: James R. Osgood and Company, 1872), 460.
60. Gillian Gannon, "Mentoring: How can it benefit our careers and what does it take to foster a mentoring relationship," Advancing professional development with mentoring, Sustainable Energy Authority of Ireland, March 25, 2019, https://www.seai.ie/blog/women-in-energy-2019/.

thought. Plato's approach to seeking deeper truths was inspired by the dialogue and questioning methods he learned from Socrates.

+ In Matilda Cuomo's book, *The Person Who Changed My Life: Prominent People Recall Their Mentors*, CBS anchorman Walter Cronkite shared how he was inspired and encouraged by his high school journalism teacher, Fred Birney.

+ In 1934, it was the fiery revivalist Mordecai Ham who first preached the gospel to a young Billy Graham and began a mentoring relationship that would last for decades.

You might say Arthur, Socrates, Fred, and Mordecai were successful talent scouts. They saw something in their protégés and took that next important step to point out their potential and possibilities.

The Bible provides several examples of mentors and mentees including Moses and Joshua, Eli and Samuel, Naomi and Ruth, and Elizabeth and Mary.

One discipling relationship in the New Testament stands out as a clear model for mentoring. Paul met Timothy on his second missionary journey, and their relationship grew to the point that Paul called Timothy *"my true son in the faith"* (1 Timothy 1:2).

In Acts 16 we see that Paul's key strategy as a mentor was simply including Timothy in what he was already doing. Paul also charged Timothy to pass what he had learned to others: *"You then, my son, be strong in the grace that is in Christ Jesus. And the things you have heard me say in the presence of many witnesses entrust to reliable people who will also be qualified to teach others"* (2 Timothy 2:1–2).

To check the box for this chapter, consider how your best chance at making the world a better place might involve taking on an apprentice, recruiting volunteers, identifying an eager student, or excelling as a parent, aunt, or uncle. Can you do that? It begins by proving yourself worthy of respect and earning the right to be heard. Your engaging words and wise counsel to a novice might make all the difference in their life.

ATTRIBUTES OF A WISE MENTOR

TALENT SCOUTS SEE WHAT OTHERS DON'T

That young person with the reputation as a troublemaker? That unassuming student who attentively absorbs everything? That pesky kid who asks too many questions? They may be ripe for coaching and mentoring.

MENTORS NEVER BELITTLE OR DEMEAN

Because you have more experience than your protégé, it may be tempting to be cynical and point out flaws. Hold back on that impulse. See mistakes as opportunities. See crazy ideas as game-changing innovations. Always see the potential.

MENTORS ANTICIPATE REPLICATION

Individuals who are motivated and empowered tend to motivate and empower others in turn. The result is not merely steady and incremental growth but rather transformative results that are exponential and sustained.

MENTORS ARE FOREVER REMEMBERED BY THEIR PROTÉGÉS

Even if the world doesn't know your name, you won't be forgotten. "*Remember your leaders, who spoke the word of God to you. Consider the outcome of their way of life and imitate their faith*" (Hebrews 13:7).

Note that mentoring and encouraging are different. For sure, be an encourager for any and every apprentice. At the same time, be selective about identifying individuals for sustained, intentional mentorship. Take the time needed to listen, pray, discern, and invite.

☑ CHECKING THE BOX

At the end of their earthly lives, mentors may not get their names in the history books, but their impact is never forgotten. Plus they have the satisfaction of knowing where the credit and honor truly belongs. They never say, "Look what I did." Instead, they follow the instruction of 1 Corinthians 1:31, *"Let the one who boasts boast in the Lord."*

TO PONDER OR SHARE...

☐ 1. Did you have a mentor—even for a short season?

☐ 2. Does it help to think of being a talent scout as the first step in being a mentor?

☐ 3. Which is a more crucial element in mentoring: instruction or relationship?

☐ 4. Should it be seen as regrettable or acceptable when a mentor, nurturer, and coach fails to get applause and credit for their efforts?

☐ 5. Identify two or three people in your life that you could take under your wing. How might you approach them with the idea?

36

ADMIT YOU HAVE LIMITS

"Do not think that you have made any progress unless you esteem yourself inferior to all."[61]
—Thomas à Kempis

Turning the pages of this book, perhaps you're ready to give up. While attempting to check some of these boxes, the pencil slips from your hand. You're realizing that rescuing the world—making it a significantly better place—is more than you can handle.

If that's part of your current thought process, then congratulations. You've come to a valuable turning point in this book...and your life. It's dawned on you that even your best efforts can only make incremental changes in the world.

Cases in point: Nelson Mandela, Mother Teresa, Martin Luther King Jr., and Billy Graham each impacted *millions* with their ministry and message. That number ain't nothing to sneeze at. But there are eight *billion* people on the planet, which means those spiritual giants missed quite a few folks who desperately needed what they had to offer. They left behind a world filled with mostly unreached people.

In other words, even the most righteous and influential individuals can really only do so much. When you admit you have

---

61. Thomas à Kempis, *Of the Imitation of Christ* (New Kensington, PA: Whitaker House, 1981), 61.

limits, you're in good company. More than that, you're expressing a humility that will serve you well and open the door for new connections and opportunities. Proverbs 22:4 tells us, *"Humility is the fear of the Lord; its wages are riches and honor and life."*

For most of us, that sounds like something worth shooting for. However, if you're not motivated by the promise of "riches and honor and life," maybe you'll be frightened into being a little less prideful by the prospect of facing "destruction" and a "fall." Proverbs 16:18 offers the warning, *"Pride goes before destruction, and a haughty spirit before a fall"* (ESV).

Any discussion of pride should differentiate between the many *types* of pride. There's pride when your son or daughter drains the three-pointer at the buzzer to win the championship game. That's a good thing, right? There's pride related to patriotism. If you happen to be a citizen of the United States, I hope your heart is stirred by a passionate, yet respectful, rendition of "The Star-Spangled Banner." When you reach a worthwhile long-term personal goal, it's healthy to feel a little pride tempered with humility and gratitude for the chance to channel your gifts and complete the task.

The dark side of pride leads to arrogance, selfishness, prejudice, envy, and a tendency to manipulate others while resisting to ask for help or feedback. That kind of pride ultimately leads to self-destruction and dragging down those around you. Conversely, acknowledging your own limitations provides a gateway to transcend those limits.

SUBDUING PRIDE AND EMBRACING HUMILITY

REFUSING TO ACKNOWLEDGE YOUR PERSONAL LIMITS IS A ROADBLOCK TO LEARNING

Your goal of making the world a better place will require you to gather information and increase your awareness. Knowledge is power. Set pride aside and pledge to seek answers far beyond the pages of this book.

HUMILITY PUTS OTHERS FIRST

Coming to terms with your own shortcomings opens your eyes to the gifts and needs of those around you. Consider this historic and memorable teaching from Mark 9:35: *"Sitting down, Jesus called the Twelve and said, 'Anyone who wants to be first must be the very last, and the servant of all.'"*

BELIEVING YOU HAVE ALL THE ANSWERS IMPEDES COOPERATION

You do your part. Let others do their part. Synergy is the secret ingredient to transformative outcomes.

KNOWING YOUR OWN LIMITATIONS OPENS THE DOOR TO SERVANT LEADERSHIP

Jesus had no limits. Yet, he washed the feet of the disciples and gave himself up on the cross. Jesus modeled a sacrificial love that we can emulate, a love that initiates a ripple effect reaching beyond our own personal agendas. *"Do nothing out of selfish ambition or vain conceit. Rather, in humility value others above yourselves, not looking to your own interests but each of you to the interests of the others"* (Philippians 2:3–4).

As soon as you think you have all the answers, you stop learning. As soon as you think you can do it all yourself, you stop gathering allies. As soon as you proclaim yourself to be the person large and in charge, with no one to answer to, your dominance crashes and burns.

C. S. Lewis offers an excellent definition worth remembering: "A really humble man...will not be thinking about humility: he will not be thinking about himself at all."[62]

☑ CHECKING THE BOX

It's a relief to know we don't have to do it all. The overarching point might be that recognizing your own limitations

---

62. C. S. Lewis, *Mere Christianity: Comprising the Case for Christianity, Christian Behaviour, and Beyond Personality* (New York: Macmillan Publishing Company, 1943; New York: Touchstone, 1996), citation to the Touchstone edition, 114.

opens the door to new opportunities. You're not saying, "I can't." You're saying, "We can."

TO PONDER OR SHARE...

☐ 1. Can one person change the world?

☐ 2. How does it feel to know you can't do it all yourself and you do need others?

☐ 3. Is pride a good thing or a bad thing?

☐ 4. What are the immediate and long-term benefits of realizing you have limits?

☐ 5. Are there boxes only you can check? Are there boxes you could never check?

37

COMMIT

*"The quality of a person's life is in direct proportion to their
commitment to excellence, regardless of their chosen field of
endeavor."*[63]
—Vince Lombardi

If you buy into the idea that absolute truth exists—that there
is such a thing as right and wrong—then you have two choices:
Ignore it. Or commit to it.

I recommend you choose the latter.

Don't make that decision lightly. Committing to actively
pursue God's best for your life requires you to ask some hard
questions and make some hard decisions. Do you really want to
know what the Bible says? Will you invest your whole self in the
work—mind, body, and soul? Will you put systems and people in
place to hold yourself accountable? When you falter or fail, can
you summon the courage and resilience to recommit?

Making a commitment and sticking to it can be monumen-
tal and life-changing. Ask any marathon runner or virtuoso vio-
linist. There's a vast difference between what they do and simply
jogging around the neighborhood or playing second chair in high
school. Making a commitment means you put in the time. You go

---

63. "Commitment," Vince Lombardi Quotes, accessed March 13, 2024, https://
vincelombardi.com/quotes/

the extra mile. You don't settle for mediocrity. I have a sense you already know that.

What you may not fully appreciate is that making a commitment has benefits and opens doors that most people never realize.

From a spiritual perspective, your act of commitment triggers a series of events that will bring new opportunities and open your eyes to new truths. A Scottish mountain climber and adventure writer from the last century, W. H. Murray, expressed this idea beautifully:

> The moment one definitely commits oneself, then Providence moves too. All sorts of things occur to help one that would never otherwise have occurred. A whole stream of events issues from the decision, raising in one's favour all manner of unforeseen incidents and meetings and material assistance, which no man could have dreamt would have come his way.[64]

This big idea should embolden you. When you put your trust in the Creator of the universe, He notices. He approves. And He eagerly showers you with a customized deluge of gifts. That includes newly discovered aptitudes such as enhanced decision-making capacity, a fresh ability to love, more patience and self-control, gratitude, generosity, and a clearer purpose when you get up in the morning. Not to mention a reserved home in heaven.

According to 2 Chronicles 16:9, God is watching you this very moment inviting you to surrender to his purpose and plan for your life: "For the eyes of the LORD range throughout the earth to strengthen those whose hearts are fully committed to Him."

That's right, God sees you. Which means you can take a bold first step and trust Him to direct a thousand more steps down a path chosen just for you. Along the way you may experience an

---

64. W. H. Murray, *The Scottish Himalayan Expedition* (London: J. M. Dent & Sons, 1951), 7, https://archive.org/details/dli.pahar.2952/page/1/mode/2up?view=theater.

occasional stumbling block or narrow road, but your one-time commitment ensures that every difficulty will actually benefit you in the long run. Soon, you will no longer be surprised when God endows you with courage, strength, and wisdom at exactly the right time. Readers of the Old Testament can confirm that He will part the seas, send bread from heaven, topple walls, and suspend the sun in the sky on behalf of those who have pledged to love and serve Him.

COMMITING TO GOD'S BEST

When you check the box and say yes to God's perfect plan, you will be changed as an individual. But that decision will also make the entire world a better place.

WHEN YOU COMMIT, OTHERS NOTICE

By definition, commitment leads to change. When they see your new kindness, gentleness, self-control, joy, and peace, longtime friends will be left scratching their heads. "What's up with old grouchy pants? How does someone like that change overnight?" Your commitment may immediately get people to sit up and take notice.

WHEN YOU COMMIT, OTHER BELIEVERS FEEL EMPOWERED

Let's admit that even committed followers of Christ get lackadaisical. We forget we have work to do. Or we mistakenly conclude our previous efforts to share the gospel have fallen short, so we take our eyes off the prize. But seeing new life reminds us of our own opportunity to be part of a process that literally changes the destiny of others.

THE COMMUNITY CAN, AND WILL, USE YOUR GIFTS

The body of believers needs committed teachers, healers, huggers, singers, dancers, writers, innovators, programmers, marketers, team players, leaders, project managers, custodians, technicians, accountants, missionaries, and prayer warriors. All interdependent. None more important than any other. Which one are you?

THE WEIGHT OF THE WORLD GETS SHARED

The world is broken. That's the core premise of this book, and one of the overarching themes of the Bible. Each time someone commits to being part of the solution, the load becomes a little bit lighter for each dedicated worker.

According to the Center for the Study of Global Christianity at Gordon-Conwell Theological Seminary, there are 2.6 billion Christians worldwide at the time of this writing.[65] If you've ever wanted to be part of something bigger than yourself, the commitment we're talking about makes great sense. Nonetheless, making a commitment to God is not a group resolution. It's a personal choice made in a single moment in time.

That decision requires you to acknowledge how your sinful condition separates you from God, understand that Jesus's sacrifice on the cross paid the price for your sins, and accept that free gift of grace. No pastor, parent, or partner can do it for you. An army of supporters and cheerleaders are most welcome, but that is one box that only you can check for yourself.

☑ CHECKING THE BOX

Commit, and you will forge more than a partnership with billions of believers. You gain a brother in Jesus, an advocate in the Holy Spirit, and a Father who created the entire universe.

TO PONDER OR SHARE…

☐ 1. Have you made a decision for Christ? Would you like to? You can do that right now.

☐ 2. Who will be most surprised when you commit your life to following Jesus?

65. "Status of Global Christianity 2024," Annual Statistics, Gordon-Conwell Theological Seminary, https://www.gordonconwell.edu/center-for-global-christianity/resources/status-of-global-christianity/.

☐ 3. Who will you tell first? And how do you suspect your life may change?

☐ 4. Making a life commitment to God will give your life purpose, meaning, and deep satisfaction, while also making it more difficult. Are you ready for that?

☐ 5. If you're making a first-time decision, you are encouraged to take an inventory of your life as it is now, so you can be aware of changes in the coming weeks, months, and years. Make sense?

38

NEVER FAIL

"Love does not rule, but directs, and that is better."[66]
—Johann Wolfgang von Goethe

I don't hate too many things, but I hate when Christians are accused of being haters.

As you are probably aware, the culture wars have labeled the pursuit of Christian ideals as bigotry, intolerance, misogyny, classism, nationalism, homophobia, and other words that are the exact opposite of why God sent his Son to the world.

> *For God so loved the world that he gave his one and only Son, that whoever believes in him shall not perish but have eternal life.* (John 3:16)

If God loved the world so much that He sacrificed His son, where does this false narrative accusing Christians of harboring hate come from? And why does this divisive and damaging attitude seem to be on an upward trend?

We could blame the media for showcasing any disparaging footage they find of a pastor or ministry leader. Media outlets seem to take delight in broadcasting damaging sound bites to create a

---

66. Johann Wolfgang von Goethe, "The Green Snake and the Beautiful Lily," *Goethe's Standard of the Soul,* trans. D. S. Osmond, accessed at https://rsarchive.org/Books/GA022/English/APC1925/GA022_c04.html.

spin that fits their preferred narrative. Social media, of course, then picks up the worst of the worst and spreads those images virally.

Another factor may be Christians who choose to align themselves with a political or cultural movement, and consequently permanently link the reputation of the church with the extremes of that movement. Adding to that, celebrity influencers, including late-night comedians, seem to find special satisfaction in mocking Christian ideals and traditional values.

As a cultural force, Christians should take some of the blame. We set aside the totality of God's Word and choose to cherry-pick and emphasize single portions of Scripture that seemingly align with our wayward intentions. We fail to see the sin in our own lives and practice selective moral outrage.

Another major contributing factor to the widespread labeling of Christians as haters is the evidence of apparent conflict, rivalry, and hypocrisy within the body of Christ. We should want no part of these things and should strive to stamp them out.

Paul saw divisions and envy within the church at Corinth and wrote a long letter to address those problems. In chapter twelve of 1 Corinthians, Paul highlighted various spiritual gifts ascribed to believers, confirming that each gift is instrumental to the body of Christ. He extolled the virtue and value of being an apostle, a prophet, a teacher, a helper, an administrator, or a miracle worker. He then finished the chapter with the startling idea that, while all these individual gifts are important, there is one gift that far outshines them all: *"Now eagerly desire the greater gifts. And yet I will show you the most excellent way"* (1 Corinthians 12:31).

What immediately follows is a familiar passage that we easily endorse in broad, generic terms but that we frequently forget describes what should be *a way of life*—both inside and outside church walls. Ultimately, it's the most important box to check. Some call it "the love chapter," and it's the single most critical reminder for how to make the world a better place:

If I speak in the tongues of men or of angels, but do not have love, I am only a resounding gong or a clanging cymbal. If I have the gift of prophecy and can fathom all mysteries and all knowledge, and if I have a faith that can move mountains, but do not have love, I am nothing. If I give all I possess to the poor and give over my body to hardship that I may boast, but do not have love, I gain nothing.

Love is patient, love is kind. It does not envy, it does not boast, it is not proud. It does not dishonor others, it is not self-seeking, it is not easily angered, it keeps no record of wrongs. Love does not delight in evil but rejoices with the truth. It always protects, always trusts, always hopes, always perseveres. Love never fails.   (1 Corinthians 13:1–8)

THE GLORY OF LOVE

LOVE SETS US APART

Love tells the world who we are and whose we are. *"By this everyone will know that you are my disciples, if you love one another"* (John 13:35).

LOVE HAS A RANGE OF VARIATIONS

Don't be confused by the differences between romantic love, brotherly love, familial love, self-love, selfless love, love for the Creator, and love from the Creator. That said, remember that any love that "rejoices with the truth" is always the right choice.

LOVE EVEN MAKES BAD STUFF BETTER

Authentic love is the best antidote to our own sinful condition. *"Above all, love each other deeply, because love covers over a multitude of sins"* (1 Peter 4:8).

GOD IS MORE THAN JUST THE SOURCE OF LOVE

God is love. Without Him, there is no love. *"Whoever does not love does not know God, because God is love"* (1 John 4:8).

Authentic followers of Christ should have the market cornered on love. Consider 1 John 4:11–12 to be an instruction, a promise, and a warning: *"Dear friends, since God so loved us, we also ought to love one another. No one has ever seen God; but if we love one another, God lives in us and his love is made complete in us."*

Loving others requires us to show them how our faith gives purpose and meaning to our own lives and to invite them to join us in a relationship with Jesus. Love would never let someone wallow in patterns of sin and destruction. Love reveals a better way.

☑ CHECKING THE BOX

Love never fails. Which means every sincerely loving action we make draws someone closer to the kingdom of God.

TO PONDER OR SHARE...

☐ 1. How is it possible that those who don't know God often claim to have cornered the market on love?

☐ 2. How often would your words and actions be considered unloving?

☐ 3. When someone in your circle of influence is sinning, what's the best way to love them?

☐ 4. In this season of life, do you feel more hated or more loved? How might you respond?

☐ 5. Consider the traits of love described in 1 Corinthians 13. Are you patient and kind? Do you choose not to envy and boast? Do you refrain from pride, dishonoring others, selfishness, anger, and keeping record of wrongs? Do you rejoice in the truth and always strive to protect, trust, hope, and persevere?

39

DON'T GIVE UP

"I've read the last page of the Bible.
It's all going to turn out all right."
—Billy Graham

Unless you are clueless about history, you can easily anticipate the endings of movies like *Lincoln, Titanic,* and *Apollo 13.* The president's assassination, the ship's sinking, and the astronauts' safe return don't come as surprises. Still, there's plenty of drama leading up to those final scenes.

The same can be said of life. And, for that matter, the lifespan of the entire planet. There's no shortage of drama—but the endgame has long been decided.

The Bible tells us, *"Dear friends, do not be surprised at the fiery ordeal that has come on you to test you, as though something strange were happening to you"* (1 Peter 4:12). For those who have trusted Jesus, we know that *"our citizenship is in heaven. And we eagerly await a Savior from there, the Lord Jesus Christ"* (Philippians 3:20).

It's comforting to know that, however your life unfolds, God's plan is in place. For sure, crud happens: Shots are fired, and good men die. Icebergs lie ahead. Mission commanders sometimes have to report, "Houston, we have a problem." Still, in the end, we will claim victory.

That realization should bring comfort—but it should also motivate us to keep our eyes on the prize. To never give up. We each have been given the ability and the responsibility to draw others into God's grace—with our words, actions, prayers, love, generosity, and the very testimony of how we live.

This call reaches us in our healthiest days (when we feel on top of the world) and in our days of deepest sorrow (including the final moment when we draw our last breath). Our spirit need never falter. The more people we reach, the more glory is generated.

> *As God's grace reaches more and more people, there will be great thanksgiving, and God will receive more and more glory. That is why we never give up. Though our bodies are dying, our spirits are being renewed every day. For our present troubles are small and won't last very long. Yet they produce for us a glory that vastly outweighs them and will last forever!*
> (2 Corinthians 4:15–17 NLT)

Go ahead, if you must, and list all the disappointments of this world. From abortion to mass shootings. From gender confusion to the disintegration of the family. That list could even include all the things that were illegal not so long ago but are now a normal— or even celebrated—part of mainstream American life. Stack that anguish as high as you can imagine!

And now, hear this: That stack is a trifle compared to the unending glories that wait for us. (And never forget that those glories are still available to currently lost individuals whom we can help lead into a relationship with Christ!)

Another reason not to give up is the equally impressive list of astounding gifts from the Creator we can enjoy here and now. From puppies to redwood forests. From starry skies to the laughter of grandkids. From first snowfalls to placing the last piece of a jigsaw puzzle. Wonderfully so, even the grandest list of joys found in this life still pales next to the glories that wait for us and for those whom we help lead to Jesus.

DON'T GIVE UP ON GOD'S ASSIGNMENT FOR YOU

Keep checking the boxes God has selected just for you. Never give up on the quest to make the world a better place. And never forget that, although the world is broken, we have access to joy around every corner. Beyond that, we're not home yet, and while we're here, we have an assignment that should be keeping us busy.

TO GIVE UP SUGGESTS WE LACK TRUST

Agonizing over this world or denying the existence of hope suggests that we think God is not in control, that God doesn't love humanity, and that we're adrift in this fallen world and all on our own.

TO GIVE UP BELITTLES OUR PURPOSE

We've been commissioned to love and to receive love. Giving up means we've failed at least half of that responsibility.

GIVING UP BECOMES DANGEROUSLY HYPOCRITICAL

You've spent much of your life standing up for things that really matter. Truth. Freedom. Respect. Justice. Love. If you give up on those virtues, you're saying they're not important.

JESUS DIDN'T GIVE UP

On the cross, when Jesus said, "It is finished," He was doing the opposite of giving up and admitting defeat. At Calvary, with those words, Jesus claimed victory over death. What looks like failure in the eyes of the world actually ushers in a new understanding of what matters; fresh hope to begin again; and victory that opens the gates of heaven.

Satan is in denial about the ultimate showdown between good and evil. Armageddon is Satan's final downfall, and the question is, "Will you be on the sidelines? On the losing side? Or claiming victory?" The last chapters of the Bible suggest that our glorified bodies may be dressed in linens riding on white horses as part of the armies of heaven. (See Revelation 19:14.) It's way past time to prepare for battle. Begin today. Right here, right now.

☑ CHECKING THE BOX

> God doesn't need our help to win the battle of the ages. The ending has been written, and the victory has been claimed. Our call to arms is about sharpening our own testimony and putting on the armor of God, including the belt of truth, the breastplate of righteousness, feet fitted with the gospel of peace, the shield of faith, the helmet of salvation, and the sword of the Spirit. (See Ephesians 6:10–18.)

TO PONDER OR SHARE...

☐ 1.   Have you considered how your story ends? Are you currently living in anguish or victory?

☐ 2.   Should we put on the armor of God (described in Ephesians 6) for today or for the end times? Or both!

☐ 3.   Do you know someone who has "given up"? What can you do to recruit them back into God's army?

☐ 4.   Does the military jargon contradict your image of Jesus as Prince of Peace and make you uncomfortable? Can you see how it takes the determination of a warrior to be the ultimate peacemaker? The words of Jesus in Matthew 10:34 confirm, *"Do not suppose that I have come to bring peace to the earth. I did not come to bring peace, but a sword."*

☐ 5.   Do you find comfort in knowing the end of the story?

40

THROW STARFISH

"Do your little bit of good where you are; it's those little bits of good put together that overwhelm the world."
—Desmond Tutu, attributed

Even if you check every box God has set in front of you, it will never be enough. One person can't save the planet.

But you can do something. You can make the world a better place. It's really as simple as taking to heart the lesson of this brief parable:

> Early one morning, an old man was walking along a beach that was covered with starfish as far as the eye could see. A storm the previous night had washed them ashore, leaving thousands of the delicate creatures destined to die by midday from the heat of the rising sun.
>
> Off in the distance, the man saw a young boy picking up starfish, one by one, and casting them back into the ocean. Approaching the boy, the old man scoffed, "What are you doing? There are far too many starfish for you to make a difference."
>
> The boy paused for just a moment, then picked up another starfish and threw it gently into the tide and watched it

wash out to sea. Smiling up at the old man, he said, "I made a difference for that one."[67]

This story, adapted from the 1968 book, *The Unexpected Universe* by Loren Eiseley, has been retold in various media. It's a fitting end to this book because it perfectly captures our goals: To prompt love in action. To recognize unmet needs. To make impacts where we can. To change the world—one person, one deed, one decision at a time.

Is that something you can do?

If your solo efforts as a starfish-thrower still seem to fall short of any meaningful impact, here's an idea: Double your impact. Recruit another star-thrower.

Then another. And another. Then suggest each member of your beachcombing team recruit new members. The result will be exponential growth.

Two thousand years ago, a man named Peter inspired that kind of multiplication when the Holy Spirit led him to speak with confidence and truth. The second chapter of Acts records Peter imploring the crowds to, *"save yourselves from this corrupt generation"* (Acts 2:40).

> *Those who accepted his message were baptized, and about three thousand were added to their number that day. They devoted themselves to the apostles' teaching and to fellowship, to the breaking of bread and to prayer….And the Lord added to their number daily those who were being saved.*
> (Acts 2:41–42, 47)

The world changed that day. God used one man—impulsive Peter, occasionally rebuked by Jesus, sometimes violent, a man

---

67. Adapted from Loren C. Eiseley, *The Unexpected Universe* (Orlando, FL: Harcourt Brace & Company, 1968, renewed 1996 by John A. Eichman, III.), 88–92.

who denied Jesus three times—to begin a worldwide movement that continues today.

We're living in a different place and time, but the stakes are just as high and the opportunity without limits.

Of course, you can't do everything. But you can do something.

Don't wait for the stars to align or your mommy to give you permission. If you're waiting for some sign from the cosmos, well, maybe this is it.

Just as you are—imperfect and beautiful in the sight of God—you are fully equipped to reach down to rescue a starfish, or reach up and touch the stars.

In humility, ask God to reveal a few boxes that need attention. You can even choose for yourself which box to check first. This very day—one loving gesture, one starfish, one box at a time—you can make a difference. You will make the world a better place.

TO PONDER OR SHARE...

☐ 1. Have you heard the starfish story before? Do you imagine yourself as the old man or the boy? Or a bystander?

☐ 2. Are you disappointed that one human can't save the planet? Do you wish you could do more?

☐ 3. What are the obvious boxes already in front of you waiting to be checked?

☐ 4. Who will you recruit to help you throw starfish, check boxes, and make the world a better place?

☐ 5. What are you waiting for?

ABOUT THE AUTHOR

After a decade of penning advertising campaigns for airlines and beer, Jay Payleitner became a freelance radio producer, working for Josh McDowell, Chuck Colson, Voice of the Martyrs, Bible League International, and others. He is a popular speaker on parenting, marriage, creativity, and getting life right. Jay has authored more than twenty-five books including *The Next Verse: What You Never Knew About 60 of Your Favorite Bible Passages, 52 Things Kids Need from a Dad, The Prayer of Agur, Hooray for Grandparents!* and *What If God Wrote Your Bucket List?* He's a longtime partner of Iron Sharpens Iron and the National Center for Fathering. Jay and his wife, Rita, live near Chicago, where they raised five kids, loved on ten foster babies, and are cherishing grandparenthood.

MESSAGE FROM THE AUTHOR

If one of these chapters had a meaningful impact for you, or if you happen across another instance in which "checking the boxes" delivers a surprise, delight, or personal challenge, please let me know.

You can track me down at jaypayleitner.com.